D0360182

Empowering Parents

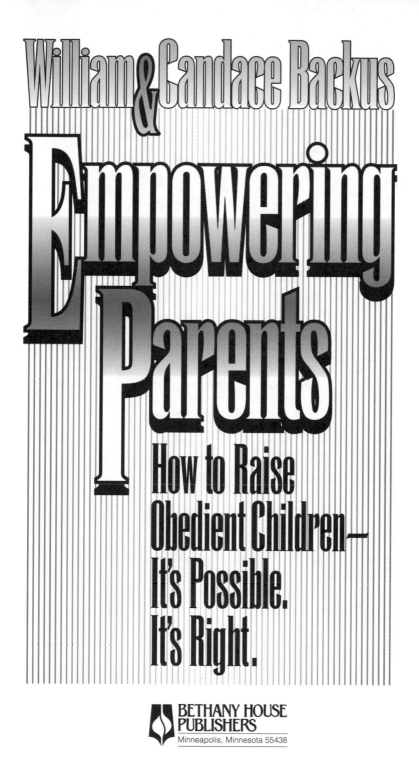

William & Candace Backus

Empowering Parents

How to Raise
Obedient Children—
It's Possible.
It's Right.

BETHANY HOUSE
PUBLISHERS
Minneapolis, Minnesota 55438

All scripture quotations, unless indicated, are taken from the Holy Bible, New International Version. Copyright © 1973, 1978, 1984 International Bible Society. Used by permission of Zondervan Bible Publishers. All rights reserved.

Copyright © 1992
William and Candace Backus
All Rights Reserved

Published by Bethany House Publishers
A Ministry of Bethany Fellowship, Inc.
6820 Auto Club Road, Minneapolis, Minnesota 55438

Printed in the United States of America

Library of Congress Cataloging-in-Publication Data

Backus, William D.
   Empowering parents / William & Candace Backus.
     p. cm.

    1. Child rearing—Religious aspects—Christianity. 2. Child rearing—United States. 3. Discipline of children—Religious aspects—Christianity.
I. Backus, Candace. II. Title.
HQ769.3.B33 1992
649'.1—dc20   91–46572
ISBN 1–55661–256–7   CIP

To Amalia, Eric, Jacob, and Jennifer

WILLIAM BACKUS, Ph.D., is a Christian psychologist and an ordained Lutheran clergyman. He is founder and director of the Center for Christian Psychological Services in St. Paul, Minnesota. He and his wife, Candace, make their home in Forest Lake, Minnesota. He is also associate pastor of a large Lutheran church.

WILLIAM and CANDACE BACKUS live in Forest Lake, Minnesota. They serve as counselors at the Center for Christian Psychological Services, St. Paul. Candace is Vice President of Minnesota Psychtests, Inc. William is a clinical psychologist and assistant pastor of a large Lutheran church.

Contents

Books by Dr. Backus

Empowering Parents
Finding the Freedom of Self-Control
Finding the Freedom of Self-Control Study Guide
   (with Steven Wiese)
Good News About Worry
The Hidden Rift With God
The Paranoid Prophet
Telling Each Other the Truth
Telling the Truth to Troubled People
Telling Yourself the Truth (with Marie Chapian)
Telling Yourself the Truth Study Guide
   (with Marie Chapian)
Untwisting Twisted Relationships
   (with Candace Backus)
Untwisting Twisted Relationships Study Guide
   (with Candace Backus)
What Did I Do Wrong? What Can I Do Now?
   (with Candace Backus)
Why Do I Do What I Don't Want to Do?
   (with Marie Chapian)

Tapes by Dr. Backus

Taking Charge of Your Emotions
Telling Each Other the Truth
Telling Yourself the Truth

A Word From the Authors

Our observation, both firsthand when we were training our four children and second- and third-hand as we've observed our friends and clients, is that the task of parenting has never been more difficult and frustrating.

On one hand, an unprecedented number of books and magazines offer parents the advice of "experts." What a rich resource! But on the other hand, so much advice and so many points of view—some of them quite alien to the ordinary parent—can be confusing and frustrating. So we hesitated long before adding to the glut by publishing another book for parents.

Yet the very thing most needed by the average parent is a simple manual that can be followed by anyone—from the single parent who is tackling a huge challenge all alone, to the committed couple trying their best to rear healthy children together. This book is for anyone interested in child-training methods that have been demonstrated *effective*.

Many "experts" make parents feel completely hopeless, incapable. We believe you love your children, that you are the one best suited of all the people and agencies on earth to instruct your own children. We know you want to discover a way of training that has proven results and is also easy to master. We also expect that you have your own ideas about how children ought to behave; therefore, what you need is some help toward reaching your own goals for your children.

In other words, this book is meant to do what the title implies: to enable you to use power you already have—the power of your own love and discipline to obtain the results you want.

As in our other books, we've used real-life illustrations. Some are from our own experience as parents, while others involve the lives of people who have consulted us. In those cases, names and minor details are changed to protect the confidentiality of our clients and friends.

A final word: Some of you may think you have already failed as parents. So have we, at times—and so have most other parents as they attempt the most challenging task a human being can undertake. Episodes of failure don't make anyone a failed parent. It is not too late to begin using the guidance in this book. If you are willing to put your less-successful ventures behind you and to experience real parent power—the power of love itself—go for it! You'll be glad you did.

Bill and Candy Backus
Forest Lake, Minnesota
March 5, 1992

I

Parenting Principles

1

Feeling Powerless

The child was so loud that no one could hear the sermon any longer.

This is so embarrassing! thought Ann to herself. *People must think we're the world's wimpiest parents.* She glanced across at Mark, who sat frozen in place, staring straight ahead—the picture of an attentive listener—acting as if he were totally absorbed in the pastor's sermon. *I'll ignore little Jeannie too,* Ann resolved. *She'll settle down soon. Everyone understands! She's only a child.*

But she couldn't help noticing the older couple in the next pew glancing again at Jeannie as she scaled the back of the pew. The child climbed over the pew and down onto the floor, disappearing under the next pew.

Others were staring at Ann and Mark now. Red-faced, Ann got up and grabbed for Jeannie, but the child crawled out of range, all the while experimenting loudly with new vowel sounds, "Oooo-ah . . . Eeee-oh . . ."

Mortified, Ann finally latched on to one squirming arm. Jeannie stopped experimenting with vowels and gave a full-throated yell. Ann tried to hush her, but Jeannie was screaming her resentment.

Meanwhile, Mark did nothing, acting as though he didn't know his wife and daughter.

Ann was mad . . . at Jeannie and Mark. She gathered the screaming child in her arms and raced for the door. The sermon had been ruined for her—and likely for everyone else. But what was she to do? She didn't have the faintest idea how to take charge. She felt absolutely powerless . . . .

Few things make a parent feel more utterly helpless than to be in charge of a child who is out of control.

For some parents, the problem may have gone on for so long that the child has become an *intimidator,* an actual threat to people around him.

"We need help. Jimmy is driving us out of our minds!" said Ralph and Jan as they sat with the child psychologist. The couple lost no time describing how their seven-year-old, during the past week alone, had pulled the cloth off the kitchen table just before supper, smashing the dishes, splashing grease all over the room. Then he threw the cat out of his second-story bedroom window, set the family car on fire by playing with the lighter, and bloodied the nose of the little boy next door. When Jan, at the end of her rope, sent the boy to his room, he flew into a rage and began destroying things.

"What can we do?" asked these demoralized parents. Understandably, they were near despair. Their son was out of their control. Would he have to be institutionalized? they asked. Could they ever hope to raise him to be a healthy adult?

For other parents, it's more a sense that their child keeps getting the upper hand in one minor struggle after another.

Our friends, the Schultzes, told us recently that Ashley, their eight-year-old, had given them no difficulties—until lately. For the past two or three months, she had repeatedly resisted going to bed. "We've tried to find out if she's afraid of something, or having bad dreams, but it seems to be nothing like that. She just prolongs the process of going to bed as long as possible. She's keeping us up till all hours. What can we do?"

This child was far from "out of control," but like many

youngsters, she had her parents stymied at bedtime.

Maybe your "power struggle" is rooted in other difficulties. Maybe you aren't discouraged at all—just looking for some strategies that will help. Are we adults *really* as helpless at the hands of our children as we sometimes feel? The answer is *no*.

Most parents come to a point where they sense they're failing, and that they're stuck in a battle they never wanted to fight with their own children.

The good news is, there *is* a way out of your helplessness and frustration. You can reshape the behavior of your children and train them up in the way they should go—*without* making your home a battleground. You *can* begin to exercise your God-given power and authority—and we know that you will see results.

Are You Vulnerable?

All parents are vulnerable, but single parents are an especially vulnerable group. A single mother can find herself suddenly alone after divorce or bereavement, or she can feel that her husband is so passive or uninvolved that she's faced with a job too big for one person to handle alone.

The parent who has to do the whole job alone can suffer tremendous anxiety. "What if I alienate the kids by insisting that they behave themselves? They're all I have!"

Another potentially vulnerable group in "blended families" are the stepparents attempting to find their place in the lives of a new mate's children. "Do I have a right," one stepdad asked, "to exert control over someone else's children?"

Why do we parents—99 percent of us included—so often let our children control us? We say we don't want bad behavior, and at the same time we don't want to alienate our kids or to inflict deep psychological wounds by making mistakes. So to avoid those mistakes, we often choose not to train our children adequately. And then we don't know what to do with the nightmare results.

Let's take a look at some of our own "inner enemies" that render us powerless.

Fear

Many parents fear alienating their children and losing their love. We all want our children to love us, and most parents want desperately to *be* loved by their children.

Some are sincerely afraid they'll do damage if they discipline firmly. They imagine their kids are little figurines of spun glass that will shatter if disciplined.

Many are reacting against their own upbringing, which entailed overly harsh discipline, injustice, abandonment, and real verbal or physical abuse.

Some feel downright guilty if their child isn't happy every moment. They believe it's their *duty* to make childhood totally happy.

Some parents fear being falsely accused of abuse. Will a welfare department child protection worker, summoned by a nosy neighbor, come to their door to investigate their parenting tactics if they insist on controlling their kids' behavior? Chances are, this won't happen, but the fear of it renders some parents immobile.

Most have simply never been taught how to shape their children's behavior, so they don't know how to go about controlling their children. As a result, many feel unable to handle their children. They imagine those bundles of explosive energy and stubborn self-will are beyond training. Even when two parents could lend each other aid, they can inhibit one another from taking action to change their children's behavior. They have never noticed the amazing amount of sheer *power* God has given them.

Parent Power

If you feel you've been an ineffective parent because you haven't known about the real everyday authority you have from God, or you haven't felt free to use it, we have news for you: You have *power* and it is right to use it. It's not just an authority based on the fact that you are bigger than your children—it's much better than sheer physical force! We want to share with you God-pleasing methods of child training that any parent can learn to apply. These methods do no physical or psychological damage to anyone, parent or child. They elicit positive feeling and convey love. And best of all, they *work*.

What You Will Learn

You've read enough so far about why you may need a program to help you. Here are the fundamental goals you will learn to carry out—our ABC's for parents:

- Goal A: *Train* each child to achieve good behavior.
- Goal B: *Correct* problems in the child's behavior.
- Goal C: *Maintain* the child's good behavior.

First, we'll lay a groundwork of understanding and then guide you through the specific steps you can follow to accomplish the goals of wise, healthy child training.[1] Therefore, we urge you to read the entire book before you begin putting the principles into practice.

After you have read and understood the material as a whole, you can go back and use specific chapters as handbooks for your own parenting practices.

To begin, we will address the feelings of guilt that most often prevent parents from achieving their child-training goals.

---

[1] We have made especially good use of the research of Gerald Patterson and his associates in devising and laying out a step-by-step strategy for working with your child. We bring it to you with the confidence that research results and our own experience have consistently testified that it is effective. We are also confident that it fosters a spiritually undergirded purpose—training up your child in the way he should go. If you would like to read some of Patterson's books, here are a couple of references for you: Gerald R. Patterson, *Families: Applications of Social Learning to Family Life*, revised (Champaign, Ill.: Research Press, 1975); Gerald R. Patterson and M. Elizabeth Gullion, *Living With Children: New Methods for Parents and Teachers*, revised (Champaign, Ill.: Research Press, 1971).

2

Guilt

Often, when we address a church or retreat audience of young parents, the discussion comes around to questions about discipline. Hands shoot up all over the room. And what most parents say boils down to this: "Help us! We *want* to train our children in a way that pleases God. But what's actually happening is that they're training us. We've lost control, and we don't know how to get them to obey us." Or we hear: "He won't do his school work . . . stay in bed . . . stop whining and nagging . . . come when he's called . . . do his chores . . . brush his teeth . . . take baths . . . stop tormenting his little brother . . . quit biting his nails. Nothing works!"

Many confide that they feel guilty for wanting to change or control their children's behavior. Isn't this a free country?

Maybe you've been feeling guilty about your desires for your children. You've heard about the "controlling parent," and you know for certain you wouldn't want to be called *that*! It raises visions of becoming a Stalin or the KGB. Yet you do want to have your children under control. Maybe you feel a trifle more than reprehensible for that!

Parents today find themselves confused because they know the Bible says they should be training their children by applying consequences to their behavior. But is that advice outdated? Legalistic? Will they do their children harm if they insist on obedience? Should they really "control" anyone? Should they actually impress values and standards on their children? Aren't parents out of line if they insist on obedience, or respect for their own authority and that of teachers and other adults? Is it wrong to train a child to choose companions on the basis of morality and values, or to eat wisely or keep a regular schedule, including a decent bedtime?

Why are parents scared these days by the suggestion that we can and should control our children? There are many reasons, of course. But one unfortunate reason is that parents so often get conflicting advice, even from Christian psychologists and counselors.

One popular Christian writer who disagrees with our advice that parents should learn to "control" their children is Kevin Leman, author of *The Birth Order Book* and other top-selling titles. He advocates what he calls *reality discipline*: giving kids choices and making them live with the results. "Reality discipline is not a way of controlling kids. Instead, it teaches kids to control themselves. That's what they have to learn if they are going to be prepared for the real world," writes Dr. Leman. Unfortunately, his discussion of "control" consists of knocking down straw men he himself sets up. No responsible authority advocates what he describes as "control." And the sole example he gives of choices children can make (what to wear to Sunday school) really has very little to offer us in situations where the child chooses to make those around him miserable, as when the child's choice is to whine, scream and yell until he gets his way.[1]

In fact, most experts in the field, even most secular writers, have moved away from the "let kids choose what they

---

[1]See the article by Dr. Leman, "Reality Discipline vs. Control," in *Parents & Children*, edited by Jay Kessler, Ron Beers, and LaVonne Neff (Wheaton, Ill.: Victor Books, 1986), p. 455.

want to do" philosophy, in favor of firm limits and steadfast discipline.[2]

Misbeliefs

So it's no wonder parents are confused—all these conflicting "voices of authority"!

And then there is another voice that erodes our confidence, a voice from within. We call this the voice of misbelief.

Misbeliefs are wrong notions in the form of an inner voice that constantly evaluates our experiences, desires, thoughts, and actions. This inner voice seems so believable, but its authority does not necessarily rest on anything like the unshakable Word of God. It rests on flimsy evidence we have gathered ourselves, from limited experience and from beliefs invested in us by others.

Here are some familiar parental misbeliefs about control:

Misbelief #1: I'm probably too authoritarian, because this idea of "parent power" appeals to me. And that's not good.

If this thought is circling in your mind, you are in constant conflict with the frightening notion that if you happen to want obedient kids, you are what some have called an "authoritarian personality"—the type of person who wants to lord it over others. But there is a very important distinction between utilizing appropriate controls because you want your children to behave properly, and being a controlling parent who can't stand it if one of the kids thinks for himself occasionally. It's true, people who are uncomfortable unless they can run everything are tyrants. But people who want to exercise sensible controls over their immature youngsters are wise parents.

---

[2]See discussion of discipline (and parental control) in the excellent resource book, *Questions Parents Ask: Straight Answers From Louise Bates Ames, Ph.D.* (New York: Clarkson N. Potter, Inc., 1988). Dr. Ames is Associate Director of the Gesell Institute of Human Development.

Second, the father or mother who desires control in order to feel big, powerful and adequate has no right to use children to prop up a weak self-image. But there is another basis for disciplining children: love.

Genuine parental love must be the starting point for any effective program of training. A desire for control and discipline can flow from real concern for the child's well-being. Dr. Ross Campbell discusses discipline and control as secondary to parental love in his book, *How to Really Love Your Child.*[3] Although some readers seem to get the impression that Dr. Campbell doesn't much care for parental control, it seems to us that, while he does favor parental control and discipline, he wants to address himself mainly to those parents for whom control is exercised without expressing love to the child. Those interested in more about parental love would do well to read his excellent book.

If you labor under the fear of being authoritarian, begin to replace this plaguing misbelief with the truth:

> It is entirely appropriate for me to want to control my children, because there is a major difference between wanting well-behaved kids and needing to lord it over them!

Misbelief #2: Children have all the rights conferred on grown-ups—at least that's what I've been reading.

Perhaps you've heard the theories propounded by the so-called "children's rights" movement. If these radical ideas are correct, you shouldn't discipline your children any more than you should interfere with the private actions of your next-door neighbor. What does that make you if you really get serious about regulating your youngster's behavior?

Some years ago, the world was much influenced by the notions of a theory called *psychoanalysis.* Books published on parenting, Alexander Neill's *Summerhill,* for example, recommended allowing youngsters to do whatever they

---

[3]Dr. Ross Campbell, *How to Really Love Your Child* (Wheaton, Ill.: Victor Books, 1977).

chose, even if adults should find the resulting mayhem inconvenient.[4] If parents obeyed these theories, their developing children would likely grow up without neurotic damage, according to Neill.

Although few writers today advocate such total parental abdication, *authority* still has something of a bad name. To some extent, this is deserved. Human authorities often abuse their power, to the hurt of people under it. The *authoritarian personality*, as defined by T. W. Adorno, has been well researched and shown to correlate with many undesirable features.[5] Consequently, notions of *authority, control* and *obedience*—perfectly valid from a biblical perspective—often become associated with such unwelcome traits as being *dogmatic, bigoted, opinionated, inflexible, reactionary, right-wing* and *fascist.*

Is Authority Awful?

As a result of misused authority, even legitimate use of loving authority may appear suspect. Therefore, some specialists in child psychology advise parents against any controls on their children's behavior. A fairly typical media event, by way of example, was a TV appearance by psychologist Joyce Brothers. Dr. Brothers offered advice at the beginning of the vacation season on how to travel in a car with children. She suggested bringing plenty of materials to keep the youngsters interested, and urged the traveling parent to involve himself in entertaining the kids. It was useful and interesting counsel, but we noted that Brothers never once mentioned the possibility that a parent might

---

[4]Alexander Sutherland Neill, *Summerhill; A Radical Approach to Child-rearing,* foreword by Erich Fromm (New York: Hart Publishing Co., 1960). As Neill's own title asserts, this book is radical. Most experts nowadays do not agree with Neill's granting to children absolute liberty to do whatever they choose, even if it's destructive! But some do. And others, though they may not go to the lengths Neill advises, believe that the less discipline children receive from their parents, the better. A closely related myth commonly propounded is that parents are not the best people to rear their children, and that it might be far better to let professionals do the job for them.

[5]T.W. Adorno et al., *The Authoritarian Personality* (New York: Harper, 1950).

simply say, "Please sit in your place and be quiet for a little while."

Shying away from authoritative intervention is characteristic of many current books on dealing with children. It's as if writers are nervous about advocating the use of legitimate parental authority. Instead of using authority and expecting obedience, parents are urged to entertain, arouse interest, understand, provide distraction, and even consult and negotiate with children.

Popular author Vicky Lansky advises parents about handling a child's unpleasant habits of back talk and biting: "Offer an alternative behavior such as biting a stuffed animal," she counseled a troubled mother.[6] There can be little objection to such advice in and of itself. We wonder, though, if Lansky has actually tried it and found it effective. However, even if it "works" (and we have doubts), no amount of such alternative-offering can teach children not to bite people, or teach them that biting another person is unacceptable.

Likewise, British psychologist Penelope Leach advises, "Toddlers can't control themselves when they're having a tantrum. Your son probably can't hear you when he's in the middle of a tantrum, so don't bother arguing with him."[7] But whether toddlers are totally unable to control themselves when having tantrums is debatable. And the impression that may be left by such advice is, you can't or shouldn't do anything about intervening in a child's tantrums—and that impression is definitely false. You *can* train your child not to have tantrums, and later we will discuss a way of doing so.

As counselors, parents and grandparents, we refuse to buy the flawed "children's rights" perspective just because it is the popular cry of the moment. Instead, we stand firmly on the side of teaching children what is *right* and what is *wrong*. It is morally right for parents to discipline and control their children. It is not abusive to insist that children

---

[6]Writing for Prodigy, a computerized service of Prodigy Service Company, White Plains, New York.

[7]Prodigy Service. See note 6.

obey, even when they don't want to.

Quickly, we must add this warning. We don't believe it is all right for a parent to abuse his children, beat them cruelly, or use children to prove that the parent is big enough to kick somebody around. But these misuses of parental authority give no reason for other parents to abdicate and act as if their children are constituents in a democracy. Children are immature and naive, not wise persons with an innate knowledge of right and wrong, good and bad. They don't automatically make correct judgments about what's good for them or what they ought to do. God has given them parents precisely because they need guidance and supervision during formative years. Their rights include the right to be taught discipline, self-control, and wisdom.

When faced with conflicts about children's rights and privileges, tell yourself:

> Children *do* have rights, but they are not identical to the rights of mature adults. For instance, they have the right to parental guidance, discipline, and wisdom, not the right to make all decisions for themselves.

Misbelief #3: If I want to control my children's behavior, I'm not really loving them. Love is enough. Give youngsters love and they won't need restrictions and discipline—even some Christian experts say that.

When people say, "Love is enough for children," they can appear to be more caring than the person who says, "I love my children, but I also want them to obey me and do what is right!"

Some people do believe that loving your children means giving them affection and privileges and expecting little in the way of proper behavior. Is this really the moral high ground for parents—*soft love* and nothing else?

Patty had read in a book that punishment and strong discipline were the opposite of love. She began to tell everyone, "I'm going to use nothing but love to raise my child. I won't use discipline or punishment of any kind. Love is better. That's the truly spiritual and enlightened way."

Is there a contradiction between love and discipline, between love and punishment? Not at all! Love can indeed be soft, gentle, and soothing. But it can also be tough, resolute, and determined—even punishing if necessary. Love can inflict pain on the beloved if it's needed for his own good. Remember how, at times, God chastens us precisely *because* He loves His children, or think of the physician's painful stitches closing an open wound. There is an important distinction to be made between *soft-mindedness* and loving.

For more evidence, let's take a closer look at the family. God's ordering of the human race into families has never been revoked. According to that ordering, every human being arrives on earth as a helpless infant, living with a father and mother as a family. The idea is that this family should consist of mature, loving human beings who will care for, love and train the child in right living.

In a proper human family, the relationship between parents and children is distinguished by love, gentleness, provision and caring on the part of the parents toward the children; and on the part of the children, honor, obedience, and love toward their parents. This so-called nuclear family has been found in culture after culture to be the most satisfactory arrangement for transmission of spiritual and moral truth and values and right behavior to children. This it does as the parents insist on right behavior and the development of appropriate habits.

The truth to tell yourself about love and discipline is this:

> Love isn't always giving in and being a milquetoast;
> if I *truly* love my children, I will have the courage to
> set limits and expect right behavior even when they
> don't like it.

Misbelief #4: I'm supposed to simply feed, clothe and shelter my children, see that they get all possible benefits and opportunities—and then stay out of their way. Parents can ruin their children very easily!

The popular view is that parents are old-fashioned sticks-in-the-mud, like the sadly typical TV sitcom Dad or

Mom whose savvy level compares pathetically with that of their "with-it" teens. Evidently, writers for TV consider fathers and mothers hopelessly dumbfounded in the face of their adolescent children's infinitely superior wisdom! Films often agree with this picture of today's parents. In the smashing hit movie *Home Alone*, the bemused parents of an eight-year-old were portrayed as so dazed and confused they inadvertently went off to France without him, leaving the boy to manage by himself.

The underlying dogma propounded by secular thinkers, and seemingly accepted by many psychologists and therapists, makes this assumption: Man's nature is good, and if a child behaves badly the deviation has been caused by society. The most children need from their parents is to have all their physical and emotional needs met. Parents may feel that after they give and give, they should get out of the way so that the child's "goodness" can emerge naturally.

Let's restore the truth about parental dignity. Most parents are anything but cretins who just get in the way. Christian common sense has always agreed with Scripture: Parents have to be God's representatives to their children, designated by God himself to guide, support and care for their offspring in His place. We were meant to love, provide for, teach and shape the attitudes and behaviors of *His* children.

But the major premise really comes out of God's Word. Standing on this groundwork as you learn will make it easy for you to see with clear vision in a mixed-up world. What the Old Testament teaches about parenting is the potent ingredient that, in fact, reinforces the disciplining parents with an enduring dignity and honor.

Take a close look at this detailed instruction from God, urging us as parents to teach our offspring:

> These commandments that I give you today are to be upon your hearts. Impress them on your children. Talk about them when you sit at home and when you walk along the road, when you lie down and when you get up. . . . And if we are careful to obey all this law before the Lord our God, as he has commanded

us, that will be our righteousness. (Deuteronomy 6:6–7, 25, NIV)

The King James Version says we are to "diligently" teach our children. If you wonder whether such advice produces good results, consider it is largely because of the enduring strength of Jewish family life that Jewish culture has retained its remarkable cohesion and identity for three millennia no matter how adverse the conditions Jewish people have had to suffer.

So the truth to implant in your heart is this:

God has given me the charge, duty, and authority to discipline and train my children. He knows that my expecting good behavior won't hurt them. On the contrary, training in obedience and respect for authority will more likely produce children who achieve their full potential and survive adversity.

Misbelief #5: Isn't the idea that children should obey their parents and that parents should train and discipline their offspring an Old Testament idea? Isn't it out-of-date for Christians living under the new covenant of grace? Shouldn't I forget it, and take the lead from psychologists?

Has someone told you that the teachings of the Old Testament about child rearing are so out-of-date they don't matter? Suppositions like this are destructive to moral and spiritual life and, in fact, may partially account for the current epidemic of lawlessness in the western world.

Yes, it's true that Christians live under a new covenant of grace and are not under the law. But does the New Testament also teach Christian parents that their children must be trained for obedience and morality? Most definitely:

Children, obey your parents in the Lord, for this is right. Honor your father and mother. . . . Fathers, do not exasperate your children; instead, bring them up in the training and instruction of the Lord. (Ephesians 6:1–2, 4, NIV)

So young parents can be confident that God has appointed *them*—not "experts," not doctors, not government, not teachers—to socialize and train their children.

The truth is this:

> The New Testament teaches the same truths about the family as the Old Testament. Nowhere does it cancel God's commandments regarding the relationships between parents and children.

In the next chapter, we will look at another set of misbeliefs that unsettle young parents—wrong beliefs about the fragility of a child's spirit and the "damage" a parent's "wrong moves" can wreak on his young ones. We believe that you'll come to understand at a deeper level why you've felt hindered and frustrated in your work as a parent—and that what you're about to read will help you find greater freedom and confidence.

3

"Shaping" Children

Child psychology and our understanding of how a child's spirit grows have taken giant leaps in recent years. It is true that children are *sensitive* and *perceptive*, far beyond what most adults give them credit for. And it's also true that destructive parental behavior can have lifelong consequences for the child, and so can parental neglect. But it's not true that "one wrong move" by a parent will scar a child for life. Let's say it now: There are no perfect parents, no perfect kids, and this is not a perfect world.

In many ways, parenting *is* a trial and error proposition, though experts can give the impression that there is only one way to raise and train children (*their* way), and that any other way is pure "bunk." This is patently wrong. Mothers and fathers, heaven knows, struggle enough with lack of confidence without suffering the raised eyebrows of "child-rearing professionals."

And so we come back to our earlier statement: As Christian parents, we can begin from a base of confidence, knowing that God chose to give *these* children to *us*. We were His perfect choice for these kids, and they were His perfect choice for us.

Second, we can also let ourselves off the hook of wrongly assuming that we should somehow automatically know how to train these children "the right way." We will do far better with our children, and save ourselves a lot of personal condemnation, if we admit that we are all *learning*. As long as we are flexible and allow our hearts to be soft—to admit errors and ask forgiveness when we *are* wrong—we do not believe children will be damaged "beyond repair" by our honest mistakes. If a parent remains humble, not prideful, love will be the spiritual oil that keeps the relationship running smoothly. Children have an amazing capacity to love and forgive their parents, and this is God-given.

What continues to foul up the gears of parenting, however, are popular misbeliefs about the fragility of children. We said that children are *sensitive* and *perceptive*. That does not mean they are "easily crushed" and "destroyed for good," as some "experts" would like us to believe.

More Misbeliefs

Here are a few more of the notions that hold back young parents from establishing appropriate controls and setting proper limits on their children's behavior.

Misbelief #6: If I insist on obedience from my children, I'll destroy their self-esteem, won't I?

Surely doubts like this cross our minds all the time. And some writers, though their number may be decreasing in recent years, argue that forcing a child to keep the rules will cause him to be emotionally stunted and neurotic by weakening his self-image.

But the fact is, *truthful self-talk and right behavior are the essential groundwork for the so-called "healthy self-image" so many experts are trying to promote.* When a child—or, for that matter, an adult—knows the truth of his worth unquestionably, he doesn't need to be told constantly that he is wonderful and valuable. When his parents show interest in *him* and in *what he does*, when they give him approval and appreciation for correct behavior, he feels right about himself without the self-doubt that plagues those with weak self-esteem.

The truth is this:

If my child learns to obey and to do what is right, and I continue to show him appreciation and encouragement, he will be more likely to have a wholesome self-image than he will if I allow him to do whatever he feels like doing.

Misbelief #7: If I impose my particular expectations and standards on my children, it will damage their own ability to learn about right and wrong.

The pernicious doctrine that children should be allowed to discover what's wrong for themselves springs from the widespread belief that there is no such thing as an absolute standard of good and bad, true and false, or right and wrong. There are only "values" held by people, and values are merely preferences. Further, nothing makes our values more correct than yours. Therefore, there is no absolute. This is called *moral relativism.* Even if you don't really believe these things, their emanations may creep into your self-talk and frighten you when you consider disciplining your children.

Parents ask themselves, "Do we have a right to 'impose' our expectations on our children?" Some experts tell them that because "values are relative," parents must be positive and never negative; that they should defer to their kids; that they should be able to train without causing any pain; that they can handle kids by learning to *negotiate* with them and never crossing them. Some theorists insist that children need to be self-determining, and that they have every right to choose whatever they wish and to *decide for themselves* what they want to do. Even for today's well-intentioned parent, there's plenty in the air that can increase guilt feelings and make the job more difficult.

Yes, it's true that parents must gradually increase the sphere of freedom-to-choose for their maturing kids. It's also true that being positive and negotiating with children have an important place. But it is *not* true that children don't need to be taught right from wrong by the parents God has given them.

The truth is this:

I have a right, even an obligation, to insist that my children choose right rather than wrong actions. This is what I've been given parental responsibility for!

Misbelief #8: I can't stand it if my kids are unhappy or angry with me. If they're upset with me, it means I don't have their approval. And I need that to prove I'm a good parent.

Many parents work to prevent their children from having any negative feelings toward them—ever. But you haven't been made a parent so you can win a popularity contest! It isn't essential for parents to make their children feel pleased with them all the time.

Rather, children must be taught to *honor* their parents, otherwise they will have great difficulty showing honor and respect to anyone, including God. The fourth commandment recognizes this by prescribing that the child show honor to parents. The word used there for the honor children owe to parents is the same word used elsewhere in the Bible for the honor all of us should give to God.

Therefore, one of the very first habits to teach children is *obedience*. Obedience is first in importance because many later behavioral difficulties stem from not learning it. Showing honor to parents, as to God, involves active *obedience*, not mere lip service to it. Deeply embedded in the minds of people of every culture is the fact that obedience to parents is a foundation on which appropriate social and spiritual behavior must be built in the developing personality. When a child is properly instructed, he will obey those who hold authority in God's place. This is the first step toward obeying teachers, the law and, finally, God himself.

The truth, then, is this:

I *can* stand it if my children get angry with me. I don't have to have their approval all the time. But I do have to teach them to honor and obey proper authority.

Misbelief #9: If I punish my children, I'm abusing them. I've heard that any kind of punishment is abusive and that we should only use positive methods to train children.

There is a vast difference, not always noted by the experts, between punishment and abuse. There is a difference between inflicting pain when you're trying to teach your child, and hurting him when you're just venting your rage or trying to get even. Of course it's wrong to inflict punishment on your child just to satisfy your own desire for vengeance. Clinicians see the damage done to children by repeated vengeful punishments, and God has said that the matter of taking revenge on anyone is His, not ours. We must never use punishment, physical or otherwise, just to vent anger.

We do advocate the use of punishment when necessary. And punishment—spanking—is not the same thing as abuse. However, as we will show you later, punishment should be used sparingly. As we've indicated, other methods of training will also work, and positive training methods will very often accomplish the goal better than inflicting pain or deprivation.

The truth of the matter is this:

Appropriate punishment is not abuse. I should never use it just to vent anger or to get even, but always and only with self-control. Then it will be for my child's training and benefit.

Misbelief #10: There are no bad children, only bad parents. If I punish, my children will think they are bad people.

If man is by nature good, there would be no real need to control or shape children's behavior. Don't many intellectuals today hold that problems come from the faults of society and the social order, and that individuals, especially children, are basically innocent and good? We agree that our focus in training should be on the child's behavior, not on his person, and that it's better to speak of a child's *actions* as bad rather than to label the child. Nevertheless, the evidence, both in Scripture and in experience, makes it clear that children are not faultless or sinless.

People who insist that children are innocent and incapable of lying or any other bad behavior have failed to look at the data. In actual fact, children will occasionally coax and wheedle, attempt to trap you into doing their will, box you in, or push you to the limit. They will sometimes manipulate to get their own way, disregard the rights of others, and do what they can to make the world conform to their will. They need correction. A parent who does not discipline does not fully love his child. Often, when we refuse to discipline, we are only protecting our own emotional and personal comfort, and this can hardly be called love: It is self-centeredness.

The truth is:

> I won't give my children negative labels, but I know they are capable of bad behavior and that they sometimes sin and need correction.

Freedom to Be God's Kind of Parents

Since you have a natural *duty* to train your children, you have a natural *right* to require obedience of children. This right comes directly from God and cannot properly be taken away from parents by schools, by government, or by anyone else. But even more, parents also have the *power* to compel obedience.

Parent power is not new, nor the slightest bit strange. It's the foundation of such traits as: the ability to be committed to God and to other human beings; the habit of obedience to appropriate authority; and the joy of loving service gladly given. When these truths are held up against certain currently popular ideas about child rearing, you can see that "never the twain shall meet."

What we want to accomplish in this book is to free you to choose against disempowering influences, and enable you to walk in confidence as you joyfully carry out your calling to be a true parent to your children.

One way of describing the seriousness with which we should view *obedience* and parenting that trains for obedience is Deuteronomy 6:1–7:

> These are the commands, decrees and laws the Lord your God directed me to teach you to observe in the land that you are crossing the Jordan to possess, so that you, your children and their children after them may fear the Lord your God as long as you live by keeping all his decrees and commands that I give you, so that you may enjoy long life. . . . These commandments that I give you today are to be upon your hearts. Impress them on your children. Talk about them when you sit at home and when you walk along the road, when you lie down and when you get up. Tie them as symbols on your hands and bind them on your foreheads. Write them on the doorframes on your house and on your gates.

Agree With God's Standards and With Each Other

Child training works best when parents agree with God's standards of behavior. And where there are two or more parents or other adults exercising disciplinary control over children, they must also *agree among themselves* on the rules they will make and enforce. It won't work very well if we fight out our differences, using the kids as chess pieces in an adult game of emotional domination.

In short, the home is meant to be God's classroom. And appropriate behavioral rules will embody and flesh out morality, right and wrong, and God's commandments as we parents teach them to our children. Properly socializing children means teaching them to do what is right in the context of life today. This includes knowledge of God, of right and wrong, of the child's cultural heritage, and of the world in which he lives. It also includes acquiring skills for getting along in the world, serving others, and making a living. It means allowing for the development of skills that will help a child cope with everyday life by learning what it means to be socially effective, appropriate, and attractive in behavior and language—as opposed to repulsive characteristics. Training your child for a useful life in society involves all this and more.

Because so much is involved today in training and equipping children for life, parents must rely on others to help them, especially parents who must work at gainful employment. But day-care centers, child-care personnel, and schools *must* be seen as *agents for parents*—not as superior "experts" who know better than we do what our children need to learn. It is not their duty to skirt our wishes in order to impart their own "wisdom."

For the Christian parent, the result of child training should be that our children render honor to God, to us as their parents, to the church, and to their country. In addition, they should understand that life requires them to assign a primary place to effortful work, and to view play as a reinforcer for work well done, not as the reason for existence or the natural destiny of everyone; that they practice good personal hygiene habits; that, as a matter of course, they go to bed when they're supposed to, eat something besides hamburgers and sweets, and give love and respect to family members, friends, and strangers; that they discharge their duties to their neighbors; that they help and befriend others who are in need; that they consider the well-being of others and place themselves in others' shoes.

Unconditional Love: What Is It?

We often hear that parents owe their children *unconditional* love. The expression is confusing and easily misunderstood, though many Christian parents try to put it into practice. We believe it is a mistake to take unconditional love to mean that a parent should administer nothing but rewards, regardless of the child's behavior. Or that a parent should never have any but the most positive feelings toward the child, even when the child's behavior is offensive, disagreeable and provocative. Or that a parent should give a child complete approval, regardless of his actions.

The wrong definition of "unconditional love" creates guilt and confusion in normal parents. It is natural at times to feel no attraction at all toward our children, and good sense sometimes tells us to withhold rewards. Properly understood, the word "unconditional" does convey a solid truth about love: namely, that in this universe there is a love which loves us despite our sinfulness, no matter what awful things we may do. This marvelous love that cannot be quenched is the love of God for all of His children. The Bible teaches that we can be empowered to love others, including and especially our family members, with that very same unconditional self-giving love. But—and this is what's important for our purposes—God does not reward us all the time regardless of whether we do right or wrong. Indeed, the opposite is true: God loves us enough to train us to live as His children, to punish our wrongdoing and reward our good behavior.

In this context, Christian parents can see that their role is to love their children with the same love with which God loves them—a love that is not essentially sentimental, but cares enough to insist on right behavior *even when the child resents it*. And more than that, we are to love in a way that teaches and trains our children. This is love in action; it is far more than discipline—it is guiding, teaching, and skill-giving so that our children are equipped to meet life.

Yes, children are sensitive, but not so fragile that their spirits will be broken or twisted by discipline and training. It is the job of the loving Christian parent to mix rewards and punishment in appropriate amounts in the shaping of our children. The truth is, a child's spirit will take the shape of the container it's placed in, and by that we mean the set of principles and rules we parents place around them as boundaries in which to grow.

The problem for many parents, we find, is that they have

read lots of child-rearing books, gone to seminars and listened to multiple tape series—and still they can't seem to make effective changes in child-rearing habits. It's our experience that there is a missing "power" factor for many parents, and often that is *confidence*. Where does confident parenting come from? This is the question we'll examine in our next chapter.

II

Parenting Techniques

4

Do I Really Have Power?

What is parenting?

Certainly parenting involves much more than merely reproducing. Parenting involves mostly giving, for children come into the world with nothing and they depend on us for everything.

Parenting also involves imparting attitudes, beliefs and habits, training children to act properly. Just as an effective classroom teacher must establish control over the class in order to create an atmosphere where teaching and learning can occur, to do an adequate job of parenting we must learn to direct the behavior of our children.

God has not only given us the right and duty to do this, but He's given us proven *power.*

Our power lies in the fact that we have control over *consequences.* All behavior occurs with a view toward its consequences, and we control virtually *all* of a young child's behavioral consequences. So we have enormous power to change and shape behavior. We control a large amount of reinforcement, even with older children, though as a child gets older we have less control, so the prime time to train is when they're young. Think of it: You control all that your child needs to live—food, clothes, shelter—and all the things that are fun—toys, games, privileges, TV, permission to come and go, money. Most of all, you control the intangibles so needed by children—love, attention, affection, affirmation, approval.

We fully advocate controlling your child's behavior and shaping it by using rewards and punishments—especially rewards. Whenever you can devise a way, you can emphasize the use of *positive reinforcement* in shaping behavior.

On the wall above Bill's computer is a "work of art" captioned *PAPA by JENNY T.* (The artist has thoughtfully included her own portrait alongside her signature so there's no mistaking who she is!) This five-year-old has, in fact, drawn an amazing likeness of Bill, her grandfather, with exactly three hairs sticking straight up on his head and patches of brown hair over his ears. Grandma Candy expressed her delight to the artist one day recently: "Oh, Jenny, that looks exactly like Papa—especially those three hairs on top of his head. It's wonderful! Look at this, Bill—it's great." Bill also complimented her about the portrait. What we did, psychologically, was to provide *reinforcement*. Partially as a result of the reinforcement she's received for her drawings, Jenny has taken to drawing pictures of everyone and everything, pictures showing ever-increasing skill, imagination and intelligence. The effect of reinforcement is to influence the behavior occurring immediately before the reinforcement is received.

Contingencies and Consequences

We prefer positive reinforcement, where possible. But we believe that punishment also effectively controls behavior, and that the appropriate use of punishment will not harm any child. When you plan your parental policies in such a way as to see to it that reinforcement comes to your child after good behavior, and punishment after bad behavior, you are arranging to control contingencies.

Contingencies are regular, foreseeable relationships between the child's behavior and what follows it. If you can arrange things so that when your child obeys, a rewarding event occurs, you are establishing a stable, reliable contingency.

Some parents fear that their children will learn to demand rewards as a precondition for good behavior. "I won't obey you unless you give me something!" Yes, it's possible to overuse this technique, which some will recognize as basic behavior modification. Later on, we will be teaching you how to gradually cut back on the giving of rewards for every good behavior. But for now, it's best to begin at the beginning—and the beginning is to learn to reward desirable behaviors you're working on 100 percent of the time.

God's Law Includes Contingencies

God's law includes commandments, and it also spells out consequences for obedience and disobedience. It informs us as to God's will for our behavior, and it becomes a kind of mirror to show us our sins and the wrath of God. In this way, it serves as a check on our flesh, so that sin will not direct all our actions. So when parents provide consequences for their children's behavior, they are doing exactly as God does, for He too spells out contingencies and consequences—good and bad—for human behavior.

Notice how God's law always involves consequences: "The soul that sins shall die"; "Do this and you shall live." So the application of *contingencies* (applying rewards or punishments *contingent* or *dependent* on the child's behavior) is doing precisely what God does to control and train us as His children. We are not advocating that you discipline children by saying, "God's law commands you to do so-and-so, and if you don't He'll hurt you!" Too many Christians use God and His Word as weapons to bash their kids with. We are trying to make it clear that parents can and should provide consequences that are regular and stable enough so a child can depend on them.

The practice of contingency-based control by earthly parents is not wrong at all when it is mixed with loving wisdom. In fact, we are following the example of our heavenly Father—and that's a pattern we do well to imitate. We believe that arranging and providing stable relationships between the child's behavior and its consequences can powerfully help the child to develop and grow in a positive direction. What's more, it is precisely what parents are here for. We find strong advocates for effective discipline among most of the Christian writers on the subject. Paul D. Meier describes "how to develop your normal child into a sociopathic criminal." Among other instructions for raising an undisciplined lawbreaker, Dr. Meier, tongue-in-cheek, offers the following:

- *Never spank your child.*
- Let your child express himself any way he feels like it. He'll learn from your example how to behave. He doesn't need any discipline.
- Don't run his life; let him run yours. . . .
- Don't bother him with chores. Do all of his chores for him. . . .
- Give him a big allowance and don't make him do anything for it. . . .[1]

True, the proportion of all these things you alone control diminishes as the child grows older. Past a certain point, you begin to lose some of the power God gives to parents of younger children. An eighteen-year-old girl once came to see me because her father had attended a Christian seminar on authority in the home and on spanking children. Persuaded that he'd been lax in exercising his God-given headship by not spanking enough, he'd taken to spanking his grown-up daughter. This is an enormous mistake—destructive in many ways.

But through childhood and the early teen years, and in most cases even later, parents continue to have at their disposal considerable power. When the child begins to earn most of his spending money, when he begins to drive his

---

[1]Paul D. Meier, M.D., *Christian Child-Rearing and Personality Development* (Grand Rapids, Mich.: Baker Book House, 1977), pp. 55–56.

own car, when he finds most of his activities provided for him by clubs, schools and friends, parents will have fewer reinforcers at their disposal. But even during the teen years, parents have powerful reinforcers that they can control. For example, the child's right to drive and obtain a diver's license, use of the family car, permission for activities of various kinds, and—a big one for teenagers—*money*!

Even adults will often change their plans to receive reinforcers. One of my associates, given the opportunity to see the Minnesota Twins play a World Series baseball game, canceled all his appointments for the afternoon—a massive change of plans, involving a lot of complicated rescheduling. But because he'd been working hard, the thought of relaxing and seeing a game was so reinforcing for him, he counted the cost and decided the chance to watch his sports heroes at work was well worth the effort!

We're not saying everybody has his price for everything, but we are saying your young children will respond to reinforcement, and even your older teenagers will find it hard to pass up the opportunity to exchange behavior you want for something they want.

Do We Pay for Good Behavior?

I sometimes hear objections from parents to the use of rewards and punishments. For example:

I don't want to "pay" my child to be good.

But God promises rewards for goodness. Why shouldn't you? God repeatedly promises that He will bless us in exchange for good behavior. "Blessed is the man that does not walk in the counsel of the ungodly . . . whatever he does will prosper." "I am the Lord your God . . . showing mercy to thousands of them that love me and keep my commandments." "Pray to your Father in secret . . . and your Father who sees what is done in secret shall reward you openly." Perhaps most behavior occurs with a view toward some kind of reward. True, the "reward" can even be very crass—for instance, the satisfaction of getting revenge. Or it may be quite noble—like the sense of fulfillment that comes from helping another person. But it's hard to conceive of our doing much of anything without aiming at a reinforcing result.

He ought to do these things because he's a Christian.

You may be right. He *ought* to obey you, behave politely, do his homework, and finish all his chores purely out of a desire to please God. But by the same token, you yourself ought never to sin, since you are a Christian. But we know all human beings are sinful and need the law of rewards and punishments to check the desires of our sinful human nature. Think about this: If there were no highway patrolmen, would most people observe all the speed limits?

He should learn from my logical explanations. . . . If I make reasonable requests, he ought to obey without rewards.

Why do we think our children ought to do things because they're reasonable? We don't always do what's reasonable, do we? If we did only what's reasonable we'd probably never sin. Demanding that others always act rationally is like demanding that they be sinless. It's asking for the unreal.

I Hear Punishment Is "Out" These Days

Occasionally, people simply object to the idea of punishment.

Punishment is brutal and harmful. It doesn't work. It isn't effective.

A few writers and psychologists agree with this objection—but very few. True, some try to rear children without using punishment at all. B. F. Skinner claimed to have succeeded in raising his daughter without punishment, applying only positive reinforcement. But nearly all child-training counselors today agree that punishment is effective in changing behavior. And most agree that it ought to be used sparingly, with emphasis placed on positive consequences rather than negative—nonetheless, punishment ought to be used.[2]

For some reason, the idea has become popular that punishing criminals won't change their behavior, won't deter crime, and won't help society. The same thinking sometimes emerges in discussions of child training. But a good deal of evidence demonstrates that properly administered punishment *does* work, even with animals. Numerous experiments have shown the effectiveness of punishment for changing a child's behavior.

I don't want to punish my child because we ought to *forgive* when the child does badly. That's the Christian way.

Yes, it's true, we must forgive those who wrong us, even our enemies—and how much more our own children! But Jesus' teaching about forgiveness is not incompatible with punishment administered out of love for the child's well-being. To swat the bottom of a two-year-old who runs into a dangerous street is a *loving* act, and in no way signifies that the parent harbors unforgiveness.

My child is basically good and innocent. He ought not need punishment. Moreover, he is a Christian. So the Holy Spirit will work righteousness in him.

But your child is a sinful human being, as well as a Christian. He inherited original sin from Adam. Because children are sinful just like the rest of us, without intervention by parents, their sinful inclinations will lead to sinful behavior habits and patterns. You can observe any child's self-centeredness as he demands that others satisfy his whims, exhibits unwillingness to share, and envies other children.

It's not hard to discover sin in children. William Gold-

---

[2]See, for example, the discussion of the disciplinary style of the "authoritative parent," recommended by the editors of Time-Life Books in *Teaching Good Behavior,* a volume in the *Successful Parenting Series* (Alexandria, Va.: Time-Life Books, 1987).

ing's powerful novel *Lord of the Flies* tells the chilling story
of a company of angelic-looking English choir boys ma-
rooned after a plane crash on a deserted island. The reader's
fear and horror grow page by page as we witness the sinful
nature at work, without benefit of healthy socializing. At
last, some of the children devote themselves to hatred, su-
perstition, idolatry, violence, and finally even murder.

The child-training theories of humanistic psychology
begin with the proposition that man is basically good—not
sinful, not neutral, but positively good. Carl Rogers, for example, emphasized a positive view of human nature:

> The innermost core of man's nature . . . is positive . . .
> is basically socialized, forward moving, rational and
> realistic.[3]

The notion that human nature is basically good does not
come from the Judeo-Christian tradition but from secular
theories about man. Christianity teaches that human nature is sinful, but somewhat plastic—that is, capable of
change. Thus the child needs training with consequences
for good and bad behavior.

My Child Is Different, So Consequences Won't Work

Many authorities stress to parents how each child is different (which is true) and must be treated differently from
others (also true, to a point), and leave parents with the
impression that there are no rules, no laws of behavior that
apply to all (definitely not true). Some even hold out little
hope that children—or anyone else—can change. "It's just
that some children are born compliant, while others come
into the world rebellious. Some are bound to be nervous,
tense, anxious, while others will always have sad, sorrowful
dispositions." According to these folks, genes do it all.

Others will tell you that the origin of indelible behav-

---

[3]C.R. Rogers. *On Becoming a Person.* (Boston: Houghton, Mifflin, 1961).
Cited in James C. Coleman and William E. Broen, Jr., *Abnormal Psychol-
ogy and Modern Life,* fourth edition (Glenview, Ill.: Scott, Foresman and
Company, no publication date given), p. 67.

ioral and emotional patterns lies in traumatic events happening in the womb or in the early years of life. What happened in the past makes your child act the way he does. Perhaps some even add the discouraging postscript: Nothing can change the effects of the past. While this stress on individual differences may include some useful insights, and while a child's behavior may include numerous determinants, including birth order, traumatic past events and even his own moral choices, it is definitely not true that there are no rules which apply across the board.

Every Child Considers Consequences

What we want to make clear is that even the so-called "strong-willed child" acts in the way he thinks will lead to rewarding consequences. For him, rewarding consequences may be different occasionally than they would be for the extremely compliant child. But even here, reinforcement is not patently wrong. Have you ever known a teen who didn't want a driver's license? Recognition and popularity among peers? Cash? A toddler who didn't want a treat? An adult who didn't want a cash bonus? Prayer power? Inner peace?

Some things are almost universally rewarding. So the strong-willed child finds it especially rewarding to win a test of wills with an authority figure. You can use even that knowledge to reward his doing what you know he ought to do. For instance, try giving in on some smaller point at issue as a reward for his giving in on another point.

Try Offering Rewards

Jack, who is fifteen, has been arguing and manipulating for months to be allowed to stay out until 12:00 on Friday nights, rather than keep the existing rule: in at 10:00. Meanwhile, no matter what you've done, you haven't been able to get him to clean his room properly. Why not offer him an 11:00 curfew each week that his room passes inspection every day? Is it so terrible to let him win on an issue in exchange for compliance on another battlefront? We don't believe it is necessary to win every single "battle."

And on the opposite side of the coin, neither do we believe that you must permit your child to do anything he chooses to do. Freedom of choice can become a false god. While good parents will give their children abundant freedom to make choices, there are universally applicable principles for guiding human behavior. God's commandments are behavioral rules applicable to all human beings.

What we are saying is that there is something which will work effectively with all children to shape behavior. That something is *reinforcement*. Reinforcement is simply reward presented after a behavior that is to be strengthened and learned. Here is an elementary example: Our fourteen-month-old granddaughter, Amalia, is learning by reinforcement. Watch her grandfather interacting with her. He says, "What's this?" pointing to the middle of my face. Molly answers, "Nose." Whereupon he reacts with loud enthusiasm: "Good, really good, Molly!" Then, pointing to the side of his head, he asks, "What's this?" If Molly makes a mistake, Papa just corrects her. Molly loves this game. "Ear," she responds. "Wow! Molly, you're really good at this! Wonderful! Now what's this?". . . . What's going on between Molly and Papa? Why, Molly is learning by reinforcement. When she answers correctly, he gives her lots of rhapsodic praise. Some of you will have noticed, incidentally, that both he and Molly are giving *each other* reinforcers and changing *each other's* behavior. Papa is reinforcing Molly, but Molly is also reinforcing him by her replies.

We Change Him / He Changes Us

In the process of training a child, both of us are trained, so we change together. While you are working through this book, try to pay attention to the ongoing exchange of reinforcement among people. For this exchange process occurs in all interactions between people. A family is a community of people who have been drawn together and united by a Power greater than themselves for the purpose of teaching and training one another. The family is pointedly for the training of children. They must learn how to talk, when to smile, and how to do right instead of wrong.

In fact, we do train one another. Our children use reinforcement to train us too, and we may not even be aware that this training is going on.

All Unawares, We Train One Another

Mothers and fathers can unintentionally train kids to have tantrums, whine, cry, steal, lie, disobey, interrupt others, and play with matches. We can do this by giving in, by giving attention, and by otherwise bestowing reinforcement without noticing we're doing it. Unfortunately, we parents are sometimes unaware of the behaviors we are teaching by reinforcement.

Parents are also unaware that their children have trained them. How? Sometimes the kind of interaction we observed between Amalia and Papa involves mutual shaping of behavior for good. But sometimes a child trains his parents to threaten, nag, carp, criticize, and yell. Watch the progress:

Alan: (looking up from his paper to see what eight-year-old Jordy is doing): Please turn off the water and stop playing in the sink, Jordy.

(louder now): Jordy? Can you hear me? You're getting all wet. Turn off the water.

(now yelling): Jordan William Turner, you turn off that water and get down from there this minute or I'm going to spank you!

(shouting at the top of his lungs): *Jordy!* If you don't turn that water off this minute, you're going to be one very sorry little boy!

Jordy finally turns off the water, gets down and goes to find his blocks. Alan resumes reading his paper, feeling good because Jordy has obeyed him.

Can you see how Jordy has trained his father to shout and threaten? If you haven't figured it out yet, please notice that he ignores his father's polite request, ignores his yelling and his first threat. However, Jordy finally obeys after Alan shouts his threats at the top of his lungs. By his obedient compliance, Jordy has rewarded Alan for his behavior. Unless Alan makes some changes in his own approach to these issues, Jordy will continue to do as he chooses. Until then, Alan's shouting and threats will reach the precise level of intensity Jordy knows he must reinforce. Like most children, he *will* obey just *before* the pain comes. By doing so, he is training his father to shout and threaten.

What We Teach by Counting to Three

Some counselors have advised parents to explain to their children that they will give three warnings before obedience is required. You may have been taught to say, "You must obey me after I count to three, or after I tell you the third time, or you will suffer serious consequences." But notice that what these advisors are teaching parents is to train their children to wait for three requests, or till the count of three, before obeying them. Why would anyone want to teach that, when it is just as easy to teach the child compliance after one request without arguing, complaining, or procrastinating? Think about it.

Parent Power Unlimited

You already have an enormous amount of behavior-changing power. You are not hamstrung. You should, from reading this chapter, have the insights to look around you and see all behavior occurring in view of reinforcement: safety, health, money, love, companionship, amusement, attention—all of them are rewards for which people strive day after day. Usually, they are partly successful, but almost never do they achieve everything they want. Children too are behaving all the time in view of rewards they foresee coming to them as a result of their actions.

The interesting fact about parenthood is that you, as a parent, have been given by God not an impossible job but the proper love, authority, and power to shape your children's behavior. We want you to think of all the reinforcers at your disposal for accomplishing this. So we'll be reading about them in ensuing chapters. And we want you to have the confidence to use reinforcement and punishment as needed to do the job God has assigned to you.

5

Reinforcement Made Clear

From what you've read so far, you will understand that we are enthusiastic about the successes of parents who understand how reinforcement empowers them. Most important in this is our belief that the law of reinforcement and punishment was built into the makeup of every human being.

We can tell you from our own experience and from the results of numerous experimental studies by others that both reinforcement and punishment will empower you for success at your important task.

Reinforcement Works!

Shortly after the two of us were married, we obtained custody of Bill's four children, and Candy became an "instant parent," though she was very young and inexperienced. (We prayed a lot.) Very soon, with what we see as divine guidance, we began systematically applying the principles of reinforcement to control and shape the children's behavior.

When one of them decided to leave her room untended

for months at a time; when another elected to spend the dinner hour glaring at us in stubborn silence; when a child dared us to make him obey; when still another stored dirty dishes under her bed until they literally turned green with mold—we applied the principles we want to convey here.

We succeeded pretty well. And, wonder of wonders, our children's behavior usually did turn out according to plan.

Yes, We Tried That Once. . . .

We have often suggested to other parents that they try reinforcement-based methods for empowering their efforts at parenting, methods we found very effective and, for the most part, pleasant to use. But some of our friends and clients have responded unenthusiastically. Others have told us, "Well, we tried that and it didn't work."

Gerald Patterson, one of the leading experts on the application of consequences in family life, and his co-workers at the Oregon Research Institute set out to help parents of teenaged delinquents gain control over their offspring. They quickly learned that when the program didn't produce desired results, the problem was nearly always due to the parents' failure to carry it out as planned. These clinicians telephoned the parents *every day* to check on the program, attending to *how* they were working the program. Results skyrocketed to an approximately 67 percent success rate. Remember, this rate of success was achieved with hard cases, delinquent and often aggressive adolescents![1]

We can't telephone you every day. But you can prompt yourself if you know what to do and how to do it. So we have determined to make clear everything you need to put reinforcement to work for you as well as it has worked for us and our clients.

God's Built-In "If . . . Then"

Much of God's creation runs by the law of reinforcement: It's a built-in "If . . . then." If you exercise regularly,

---

[1]G.R. Patterson, J.B. Reid, R.R. Jones, and R.E. Conger, *A Social Learning Approach to Family Intervention, Volume I, Families with Aggressive Children* (Eugene, Ore.: Castalia Publishing Company, 1975).

you'll be reinforced by feeling less depressed, less anxious and more energetic. If you go to work as you ought to, you are reinforced with a paycheck. If people treat other people well, they will probably be treated well by others. If you make a real effort, you will be more likely to succeed. People who honor their parents will tend to live longer than those who don't. The law of reinforcement is heaven's "If . . . then" ingrained into the rhythms of created life on earth.

What do we mean by *reinforcement*? What exactly is this marvelous law? Well, when psychologists write it in symbols, it looks like this:

$$R \rightarrow S^R \rightarrow R\uparrow$$

R stands for a *response*, a behavior, like obeying a parent's request.

S^R stands for a *reinforcer*, an event that rewards the person who did the obedient deed, like the pleased parent's praise and appreciation. A reinforcer is an event that *follows immediately after and strengthens a behavior.*

♠ stands for "goes up" or "increases."

So the law of reinforcement, translated into plain English, says this:

If a behavior (R) is followed immediately by a reinforcing consequence (S^R), the probability of that behavior occurring again is raised.

In practice, this means that each time your child does something good and you make certain he experiences immediate positive consequences, you make it more likely that he will do the good thing again. Good habits can be formed, take root, and grow very strong through numerous repetitions of this sequence:

- *Event #1:* The child does something good like coming immediately when he's called, or brushing his teeth without being told, or feeding the dog without a reminder.
- *Event #2:* The empowered parent rewards child with

smile and hug or M&M's or special permission to stay up later.

• *Event #3:* Now the probability that child will repeat the good action is greater than before.

This point is so important, we want to give you a few more examples to illustrate it. We've already mentioned a couple of concrete illustrations of reinforcement at work in our own family with the story of Molly's naming things and Jenny's artwork. Here we'll look at some samples of the use of reinforcement to strengthen socially appropriate and morally correct behavior.

Rhonda Learns to Say "Please"

Four-year-old Rhonda was learning how to make requests appropriately. We suggested that her parents reinforce her every time she used "please" in connection with her requests. We also suggested they use what are called "social" reinforcers like praise rather than tangible reinforcers like candy, food, money, or toys.

They explained to Rhonda that they would like it very much if she would ask for things by saying "please," and they rehearsed with her. "Here's how you would ask if you wanted a glass of water: 'Please, may I have some water?' Now you try it, Rhonda."

"Please, may I have water?" said Rhonda, enjoying the game and the attention.

Observe carefully what Rhonda's parents did next. Her father served her water, and both of them enthusiastically hugged her and praised her. "That's it! That was wonderful—just what we want you to do every time you want something," they cheered. "Now suppose you want a cracker. What would you say?"

"Please, may I have a cracker," said Rhonda, thrilled with herself.

Again, both parents respond energetically, actually giving her a cracker. "Wow! You got it! Wait till we tell Grandma and Grandpa what you're learning to do." Again, this was accompanied with smiles or hugs or both.

Rhonda and her parents played this "game" a few more times. Would Rhonda remember how to make a request when she really wanted something? As a matter of fact, she didn't. That night at the supper table she fell back on old habits.

"Want some milk," she demanded.

Her mother nearly complied without thinking, because she had old habits to break, too. Had she done so, she would have rewarded Rhonda for her old habitual way of making requests. Just in time, she caught herself. "Remember how you learned to ask, Rhonda?" said her mother. "Please, may I have some milk," the little girl said, recalling her lesson of the afternoon. Again, both parents remembered *their* part of the lesson. They commended her ardently as Mom poured the milk. Within a week, Rhonda was saying "please" and "thank you" without prompting. And as time went on, because her parents made it a point *never* to reinforce requests made improperly and *always* to reinforce requests made properly, Rhonda learned to say please without even having to think.

Why Can't Mark Tie His Own Shoes?

The Bensons asked us for help recently. Their son, Mark, age six, seemed to them to be slow at learning coping skills, though he was quite intelligent. Among other problems, Mark couldn't tie his own shoes and showed no interest in trying. This was quite mysterious, since Mark was in all respects an intelligent, happy child. We asked if they would observe carefully all that was said and done at shoe-tying time in their home, and to keep a careful record. One week later, we looked at their record of the interactions between Mark and his parents over shoe-tying.

Every day, at about 7 A.M., a scene like this occurred:

Mark had dressed himself and put on his shoes. "Mark, try to tie your shoes," said Helen, his mother.

"I can't," replied Mark, unconcerned.

"You look terrible with your shoestrings flapping around like that."

"I can't tie them," repeated Mark absently, as he began playing with a toy.

"Oh, all right, then, I'll do it. We can't have you running around with your shoes untied. They'll come off."

Twice, Larry had tried to teach his son to tie his shoes. Those scenes went something like this:

Dad approached his son. "Mark, it's time you learned to tie your shoes. Come here and I'll show you how to do it."

Mark replied, "I can't tie them."

"Come here, Mark," said his father in a tone that meant business. "Sit on my lap."

Mark sat.

"Now, watch while I untie this shoe and tie it again for you. See? That's how you do it. You try it."

Mark halfheartedly manipulated the laces, insisting, "I can't do it. I can't."

After a few more such attempts, Larry, frustrated, retied Mark's shoe and gave up.

After analyzing the record, we decided Mark was not interested in learning to tie his shoes because (1) his parents did it for him, so why should he do it? (2) when he did make some effort to learn to tie shoes, his parents didn't reinforce him for his efforts, and (3) Mark's parents inadvertently reinforced him for *not* tying his shoes by giving him extra attention and caring behaviors when they saw him with untied shoelaces.

We suggested the following prescription for Mark's parents: (1) *Never* tie Mark's shoes for him again, no matter what. Even if he walked around with shoelaces flapping, let him. (2) If Mark made any effort to tie his shoes, successful or not, they were to show great enthusiasm, pleasure and pride in his efforts. (3) They were to give Mark no attention whatever for loose shoelaces. But if he made any move to tie his shoes, they were to respond with enthusiasm. Never remark again on the loose laces. (4) If Mark did not show spontaneous interest in tying his own shoes within a week of carrying out the above three points, we would introduce tangible reinforcers temporarily to get him started.

One week later, Mark had not even tried to learn to tie his shoelaces. Larry and Helen had kept their part of the bargain, and were unhappy with their son's inertia. "I'm not surprised," said Larry grimly, "he's so stubborn!"

"Well, what does he like a whole lot?" asked Bill.

"I can't think of anything," Larry complained. "He gets everything he wants now."

"No, he doesn't," Helen piped up. "He *would* if you had your way. But I won't let him have everything he wants by any means."

"What does he like that you won't let him have, Helen?" asked Bill.

"Well, he loves chocolate chip cookies, but I know they're not good for him, so I don't have them around at all," responded Helen. "Another thing he just loves is MacDonald's cheeseburgers, but he doesn't get those very often."

"Would you be willing to take him for a cheeseburger whenever he makes any effort to tie his own shoes?" Bill asked.

"Realistically, it might be awkward, at 7 A.M. especially," Helen said.

"You're right," said Bill, "so maybe you'll have to use tokens. Do you have any old rubber jar rings around the house?"

When Helen nodded, Bill suggested she put five or ten of them on her arm like bracelets. She was to tell Mark he would earn a ring each time he tied his own shoes, even if he required a little help. Later, the jar ring could be exchanged for a cheeseburger at MacDonald's. She was to remind him enthusiastically of the contract before he went to bed and when he got up in the morning. Each day she was to repeat the same process, always requiring just a little more "success" at shoe-tying before giving the reward, and making sure Mark got his jar ring for small improvements. In the final stage, she was to give a jar ring only if the shoe was properly tied. Eventually, she would be able to remove the jar ring entirely, and only give praise and recognition.

Getting Tired of Cheeseburgers?

The Bensons soon tired of eating at MacDonald's every day, so they began offering Mark his favorite miniature automobiles for jar rings (two jar rings for one car at first, then three, then five). Within three weeks, during which he collected several new miniatures, Mark was tying his own shoes and receiving no tangible reinforcers. And that, after all, was the goal. We urged his parents to continue giving him a good deal of praise and attention with recognition for his "beautiful bows." They did their part well and the result was that, as predicted, Mark soon tied his own shoes every day. Oh, and about the miniature cars. Every once in a while, his parents surprised Mark with a new model when he attempted a new coping behavior, enabling Mark to collect a whole set.

Social Reinforcement/Tangible Reinforcement

As you can see from these examples, we advocate the use of *social* reinforcement wherever possible, especially for training the child in socially appropriate behavior. Smiles, pleased expressions, kindness and warmth, applause, special recognition, praise, hugs, and appreciation are examples of *social* reinforcers.

Sometimes it's necessary to begin with *tangible* reinforcers—privileges, a parent's companionship, exemption from duties and other gifts and entitlements—moving later to *social* reinforcement alone. Here are common examples of tangible reinforcement operating in a home. A child mows the lawn; his dad gives him $5.00. A child sets the table; Mom gives her a cookie after dinner. A child obeys a parent's request; her parents give her an extra half hour of TV tonight. A child washes his hands before coming to the dinner table; his mother offers him his choice of desserts. Candy, toys, privileges, and money are *tangible* reinforcers.

Often you can begin with regular, enthusiastic social reinforcement. But whatever you choose to use as reinforcement, do it (1) consistently, (2) enthusiastically, (3) energetically and (4) happily. Accompany all tangible rewards with praise, thanks, smiles, hugs or other social rewards, because by pairing social rewards with tangible rewards, the social rewards acquire more potency. Be sure to give rewards or points, stars, jar rings and other tokens immediately after the behavior you wish to reinforce.

Empowered Parents Discipline Themselves

Parents who want well-behaved children will find that they must become disciplined in their own parenting behavior. And they remember to reward good social behavior like the child's saying, "Pardon me" when he walks between two people who are talking; "Please" and "Thank you"; waiting his turn to speak rather than interrupting; and speaking in a moderate tone rather than whining or yelling. How can you train *yourself* to reward your child for such routine but essential social behaviors?

If it's obedience you want, then give your child attention, praise, and appreciation that is *not casual and halfhearted, but real and enthusiastic* when your child gives you a gift of compliance. Use tangibles if necessary at first, but remember to reward obedience. You will soon have an obedient child.

So you see reinforcement is power. It is knowing how and when to use reinforcement and how and when to withhold it that can empower parents. The empowered parent learns to lovingly reinforce right behavior.

Best of all, if you want to learn how to apply the power of reinforcement in your own parenting, you *can* do it.

6

"Reinforcement Didn't Work"

Reinforcement is one of those concepts we all *think* we understand—until we try using it. We find that when parents fail to get results, it's often the case that they're not using reinforcement, even though they think they are. Let's examine an example of failure and see what went wrong.

A Boy, His Dog, and His Stars

Roy and Sherrylynn Lorca had been working hard with Kyle, their nine-year-old son. Kyle had promised enthusiastically that if his parents would buy him a dog, he would feed and water it every day without having to be reminded.

"What a pipedream *that* was!" Sherrylynn groused during their initial consultation. "He fed and watered Reno for a week or two; then he started to 'forget.' We bought Kyle the dog so he could learn to take responsibility. We wanted him to learn to do his chores without prompting. To learn accountability. So we thought as long as he had his heart set on having a dog, it would be a golden opportunity. But he forgot every promise."

When Bill mentioned reinforcement, she laughed.

"I'd read about reinforcement in a magazine, and I thought we should try it. So I made a chart and bought a box of gold stars. I told him I'd give him a star for his chart each time he did his dog-care chores, and I put the chart on the refrigerator."

"What happened?" asked Bill.

"Oh, he showed some interest in the chart, and stuck with it for a week or so. But then the program started to fall apart again. I took the chart down and went back to nagging. It works better, but I'm getting pretty resentful," Sherrylynn admitted.

"Yeah," Roy chimed in, "she wants me to do half the nagging now, and I can't say as I blame her. But I thought we ought to get some professional advice or else get rid of Reno. Of course that'd be a little hard on all of us. He's worked his way into the family now."

Bill assured them there was no need to get rid of Reno, and nobody had to nag either. "I doubt if the problem will continue after you change to *real* reinforcement. The problem is that gold stars, tokens, and other *symbolic* reinforcers won't work for very long without backup reinforcement. Foil stars are rewarding initially for some children, but they have to be backed up by something that has intrinsic value to the child. Without real reinforcers to back up tokens, they'll probably become as worthless as a check you can't cash because the writer has no money in his bank account."

Bill went on to explain that many things parents try to use as reinforcers are either not reinforcing at all *to their child* or they *do not continue to be reinforcing* after a while. He asked the Lorcases what Kyle usually chose to do when he was free to do anything he wanted to. They responded simultaneously without missing a beat—"Play with the computer!"

Bill suggested they make a new chart and give stars or other markers to Kyle when he fed and watered Reno without any prompting—but with the significant difference that Kyle could use his stars in exchange for time on the family computer. They agreed to give Kyle thirty minutes on the computer for each star he earned. They both saw that the program would probably work, but only if they also with-held time on the computer when it was not earned. From now on, Kyle would have to earn his computer time by doing his chores. Roy agreed to check in with Bill by phone once a week for several months, just to report on how things were going.

For those months, the program continued to work well. Reno was getting daily care, Kyle was spending more time than ever with the computer, and had even started working on a self-instruction math program.

How to Choose Reinforcers

The point is, you must consider the question, "What is a reinforcer for my child?" It can be answered only by paying attention to your child's choices. Another way of making the point is to say that each person is different. If you don't know what's reinforcing for your child, pay attention to what she does when she has the freedom to make choices. If your program doesn't change the child's behavior, reconsider the reinforcers you've chosen.

Here is a list of *could-be's*. All of these are rewarding for many children, and any of them could be reinforcing for your child.

- riding a bike
- telephoning a friend
- reading a book or magazine
- watching TV
- making a batch of chocolate chip cookies
- riding a horse
- listening to the stereo
- visiting someone
- candy, cookies, gum, fruit, pop (or other favorite treat)
- going shopping
- seeing a movie
- having a friend over to spend the night
- money
- getting a driver's license

- using the car
- staying up a half hour after normal bedtime
- a story read by Dad or Mom
- playing or shopping or talking with a parent
- a trip to the zoo, the museum, the park playground
- dinner at a favorite fast-food restaurant[1]

What Reinforces Your Child?

What is a *reinforcer*? Most people assume they know. They might say, "Something good." "Something valuable." It is a mistake to assume something you like or think your child *should* like or *says* he likes will work as a reinforcer. Not necessarily so. If what you're using doesn't work, make sure the reinforcers you're giving really *are* reinforcing. We need to see that a reinforcer is what actually strengthens a behavior.

Tokens

The Lorcases' program with Kyle and Reno introduced you to another useful device: *token reinforcement*. Remember, reinforcement must be given *immediately* following a behavior if it is to have maximum effect, especially with younger children. A trip to Disneyland promised for next August won't have a whole lot of effect on whether a child wipes his feet before entering the house in March. A trip like that could be a fine reinforcer but—and this is the problem—how can you administer such a reward *immediately* after the behavior you want to strengthen? The answer is *tokens*.

A token is anything that can be made to stand for a real reinforcer. Gold stars on a chart can be made exchangeable for clothes, toys, privileges, trips, money, or anything else

[1]Please don't assume that because we list a number of suggestions as to what might be a reinforcer for your child we are recommending that particular activity or substance. We don't think much of the health value of eating lots of candy or having numerous meals at fast-food restaurants. But we realize that for those who want to use these as rewards *once in a while*, there is likely no harm done!

you want to make them good for. They can be given immediately, placed on the chart in the kitchen and always accompanied by a good deal of expressed pleasure: praise, smiling, and happy recognition. You don't have to use gold stars on your charts. Any kind of sticker or marks with a pencil or pen will do as well. By pairing tokens of no intrinsic worth with real reinforcers, the marks or tokens become what psychologists call *conditioned reinforcers* and acquire the power to strengthen behavior. Here's the point to remember: Tokens will lose their power unless they are at least occasionally paired with real reinforcement.

One other point about reinforcers: Any of the suggestions we've listed and others that you discover yourself may be effective for a time and then, for no apparent reason, lose their effectiveness. This doesn't mean the program won't work. It merely marks the fact that people change. So what is reinforcing this year may not be reinforcing next year (vice versa too). When a good program seems to be losing its punch even though you're doing everything absolutely on-target, examine whether the reinforcers are actually being used by the child. If not, it's time to replace them.

How Reinforcing Are You?

Here is a question for you, Mom or Dad: How reinforcing are you? Perhaps it's never occurred to you that parents, by repeatedly being paired in the child's experience with food, love, safety, and other nurturing behaviors, have become very powerfully reinforcing in themselves. You are a rewarding experience for your child—or you can be. Nothing is more important than loving your child. But love is more than a tender emotion you feel when you look at your sleeping child with his angelic face. Love is also action. It includes expressing those positive feelings and appreciation to the child. It includes letting your child sense the warmth you feel. What we're getting at is twofold.

First, don't forget that our major goal as loving parents is to get the child's behavior under the control of *social* reinforcers. We don't want him to obey you *only* when there's money, candy, or special privileges in it for him. Such things may be useful to start, but eventually he should be amply reinforced in most cases by your appreciation. So when you use tangible reinforcers, be sure to link them with expressions of your love: positive reactions, smiles, recognition, praise and gratitude.

Second, remember to use the child's name when you reward. To hear his or her name repeated by a loving parent in a pleasant context makes a great difference to your child. Some kids never hear their real names at home unless they're misbehaving.

Likewise, some children never encounter parental attention unless they're misbehaving. Only then do their parents give full attention, along with scolding and humiliation, so their experience of parental attention is always paired with put-downs. It is possible these are reasons for the negative estimation in which some children hold themselves.

So begin now to use your child's name when you express appreciation and praise for good behavior. Remember to couple your personal attention with positive emotions and reactions when the child makes efforts to please and succeed. Whatever other reinforcers you use, remember that *you* personally are the most important of all the reinforcers in your child's life.

A Worthwhile Exercise

You may not be sure of the answer to this question: How much and how effectively have you been offering your child loving social rewards? Find out:

- Get a notebook. You'll need one anyway for other records. And for three normal days, keep track of your responses when your child does things he's supposed to do the way he's supposed to do them.
- Use the record to determine your responses. Do you respond at all? Is your response humdrum and perfunctory? Excited and enthusiastic? Pleased? Do you nag or yell when your child misbehaves? Write down what you

do or perhaps what you fail to do each time. Discover whether you yourself are reinforcing your child's efforts to please you.

- Find out what you need to work on to become an empowered parent, and use that power.

7

Change Yourself First

Does it feel as if life gets so ahead of you that you're out of breath? Are you the good parent who "just can't get organized"? Maybe you're full of good intentions, or brimming over with advice on parenting from books and magazines. You try a little of this and a little of that, but never stick to any one program. Maybe you're also trying to hold a job and raise three kids, and you never have time for anything. Maybe you're a single parent, with the sole responsibility for *everything*—or you might as well be, because your spouse is physically or emotionally absent most of the time. Maybe you just plain have never been able to get organized.

A Parent Can Make Progress

Years of clinical experience in helping parents to help children have taught us this: The best progress a child makes in overcoming a behavioral problem comes when the parents make progress in getting organized enough to administer the program. When the program succeeds, we know for certain the success is not *our* doing, but is a result of *parents getting down to business and doing their work properly*.

70

When a program fails, it's usually because parents don't understand it, can't carry it out, or maybe even refuse to do it properly.

If you're going to use reinforcement, you need to know ahead of time that you *must* reinforce good behavior *immediately after the behavior occurs* and do it *consistently*. You will have to get organized enough to administer reinforcers as soon as the child does the behavior you want, and you will have to do it every time! No slipups. No procrastination. No delays. No excuses.

Why Scott Didn't Graduate

Hal and Janet Madden couldn't hide their discouragement. Their seventeen-year-old son, Scott, a senior in high school, had been cutting classes. "No way can he graduate in June," the principal warned in February, "unless he attends classes regularly from here on."

As we listened to this couple, we realized that much of Scott's behavior was now out of his parents' control. Their opportunity for shaping Scott's character had nearly passed. He'd been doing whatever he wished for years, with little or no effort to conform to his parents' wishes, and he'd suffered few consequences. Now he was, chronologically, almost an adult. If the goal was to get Scott through his last year of high school, something different had to be done fast.

"Does he have a car?" asked Bill.

"No," replied Jan, "but Hal's been thinking of buying my dad's car for him as an incentive to get through school."

"Fine," Bill replied. "Here's what you should do . . ."

Bill carefully instructed Jan and Hal in a simple procedure. They were to bring the car home, park it in the driveway and make the keys unavailable to Scott, telling him that he would own the keys and the car when he had finished his last year in school by simply attending every class. Scott was to obtain a slip signed by each teacher every day certifying that he had attended classes. The car was to be his when he had obtained slips for all classes between

March 1 and graduation day in June. Hal and Jan understood, felt sure it would work, and agreed enthusiastically.
Bill was confident this reinforcer would work with almost
any high school senior who had no wheels to call his own.

Two weeks later, Jan and Hal returned to the office for
a check on how things were going.

"Terrible," said Jan—and she gave her husband a cutting
look.

"It's not working at all," said Hal mournfully.

Bill could hardly believe it. "Did you get the car?"

"Yes," said Hal, looking sheepish.

"Did you tell him about earning it by attending classes?"

"Yeah," Hal responded, "and he was so thrilled he
couldn't wait. He wanted the car right away."

"Of course he did," Bill replied. "That's why it's a perfect
reinforcer for him." Suddenly Bill had a horrible thought.
"You didn't *give* him the car, did you?" he asked, hardly
daring to listen to the answer.

"Uh-huh," Hal replied shamefacedly. "He wanted it so
badly, and he promised he'd attend every class. He said he
needed wheels more now than at the end of high school. So
I made him promise—again—to go to all his classes. And I
gave him the keys."

Reinforcing the Child's Misbeliefs About Life

Here were parents who wanted only the best for their
children. But unfortunately, like many folks, the Maddens'
parenting was rendered nearly powerless by the misbelief
that loving and doing your best for kids is the same thing
as giving them *what* they want *when* they want it. Hal and
Jan allowed this wrong notion to control their parenting
with the result that their children controlled them.

All they actually accomplished was to reinforce Scott
for his self-defeating belief that he would always be entitled
to what he wanted when he wanted it, and that his promises
were as good as actions. But the truly sad result was that
Scott and his siblings were deprived of the training they
needed to make it in life. Scott didn't finish high school.

Without a diploma, most doors to the future will be closed for him, since other people will hardly treat him with the same indulgence he's become accustomed to.

How can a parent consistently allow the immediate pleasure of giving a child what he wants to deprive their precious offspring of the training needed to make it through life? Isn't a few minutes of the child's displeasure worth the end result to a parent informed by love and focused on long-term goals?

"Backward" Reinforcement Won't Work

You can learn from the Maddens' sad tale: *Never try backward reinforcement*. Numerous behavioral experiments have demonstrated the same lesson exemplified by Hal's mistake with Scott. Giving the reinforcer first, in the hope that the desired behavior will follow, has *no effect on behavior*. It won't work.

Roberta's Mistake

Roberta Angelo, a single parent, had her hands full with her two children, both of school age. She brought in a list of problems she'd been having with her daughter, Niki, who was eight. Niki normally ignored her mother's requests until Roberta lost her temper and screamed with rage at her daughter, at which point Niki would halfheartedly comply. We decided to focus on teaching Niki compliance before starting work on any other behavior. As a rule, it is best to begin work on one behavioral difficulty, then move on to others after the first one is well under control. We developed a plan for Roberta to give Niki a nickel every time she did what she was told without arguing, complaining, or procrastinating. Roberta was to make a point of giving her daughter at least ten commands each day. Roberta bought a few rolls of nickels at the bank, and the program got off the ground.

The first week's records showed that Niki had obeyed in the desired way 89 percent of the time (up from 52 percent before the program began). The second week's record demonstrated further success: Niki's compliance rate was 96 percent!

Roberta canceled her third appointment. Finally, after a fourth week went by, we called her to ask how things were going. "Not so well," replied Roberta. "Niki's back to her old ways. She hasn't been doing what she's told."

"What's her compliance rate?" we asked.

"Well, I haven't been keeping the records as well as I should. And I guess I ran out of nickels." Roberta admitted that she hadn't been carrying out the program consistently. She was very busy, she told us, and sometimes, even if she had nickels in her purse, she just didn't feel like getting up and going to find her purse every time reinforcement was called for. Roberta's application of the program was the problem because she failed to give reinforcement *consistently* and *immediately*.

Nancy Halstead Shows Us How

Nancy Halstead had adopted a five-year-old boy born in an Asian country. She knew she would have her hands full as a single mother, but she was enthusiastic about motherhood and was prepared to give it her best.

But little Robbie had much to learn by way of appropriate behavior. He had numerous behavior difficulties, so Nancy sought our help.

We planned a program for training Robbie, deciding together that Nancy would use token jar rings for immediate reinforcement when Robbie performed the behaviors we targeted. Robbie was allowed to exchange the jar rings for treats and privileges, and Nancy agreed to express her pleasure and to praise Robbie when she administered reinforcement.

At follow-up visits and calls, Nancy's successes with Robbie continued. And, as is always the case when the child's changes become enduring, Nancy made a point of using backups that were really reinforcing to Robbie, applied reinforcement consistently, and responded to his good behaviors with reinforcers immediately.

Reinforce Immediately and Every Time (at First)

Much experimental data shows that the power of reinforcement diminishes if too much time elapses between the behavior and the giving of reward.

Let's imagine your child cleans his room and Mother says nothing, perhaps intending to praise him, but forgetting. So she gives him no attention or recognition for doing well. A week later, she notices things aren't going so well— the room is anything but clean, and Mother is reminded of her negligence. She decides to give the reinforcement she should have given earlier: "You did so well last Saturday. I really appreciated the fact that you cleaned your room." But there won't be much positive effect from that reinforcement because of the timing. In fact, since the reinforcer occurred after the child's *nonperformance*, it may strengthen his *not* cleaning his room. Does your child hear from you only after she has *not* performed properly? Or when it is too late to connect it with the behavior? *Deliver reinforcement immediately.*

When parents reinforce children consistently, target behaviors can and will be consistently performed. Reinforce the child every single time until the behavior you want becomes routine. Then and only then should you decrease the frequency of reinforcement. Your object eventually is to maintain the behavior with only occasional reinforcement.

Moving On to Intermittent Reinforcement

Candy taught our granddaughter, Jenny, to swim. An important part of the program was for Jenny to learn to hold her head under water without fear. At first, Candy rewarded Jenny every time she got her face even a little bit wet. Candy praised her enthusiastically.

But look at the swimming lessons a few weeks later: Now, Candy praises Jenny only about once every fifth or sixth time she ducks her head. Getting her face wet is now routine. When Jenny holds her head down and kicks her way through the water, she is reinforced every time. Later these behaviors will be reinforced only occasionally.

The practice of bringing a child to the point in learning a particular behavior where reinforcement is given only occasionally, on a random basis, is one way of giving her *intermittent* reinforcement. Intermittent reinforcement builds strong behaviors, that is, behavior habits that are so deeply rooted that they are actually difficult to extinguish.

After ten-year-old John Sutliff developed the habit of setting the table for supper every night, his mother gradually rewarded him less frequently until, at last, the only reinforcement he received was that Mom would, once in a while, unpredictably, say something like, "I really appreciate the way you're setting the table for me. It's like professional work. You can't imagine how good it feels to have you do that every day! Thanks!" And even less frequently, she might add something like, "Here's a dollar. Buy yourself something you'd really enjoy munching on!" Eventually, John would set the table routinely and such reinforcement by his mother occurred only once every few months.

To Begin

Establish goals in your mind today and make a contract with yourself to carry them out when you start a program with your child. Promise yourself you will:

- Start by reinforcing new good behavior *every time*. So at this stage of the game, it would be very wise for you to memorize the self-instruction, "I will reinforce my children *consistently* every time they execute the behaviors we're trying to shape."
- Reinforce your children *immediately* when they execute the behaviors you want them to acquire.
- Later on, after these behaviors are well learned, you can work toward intermittent random reinforcement and

replacing tangible reinforcers with social reinforcers.

And finally—a grace-note: *Reward yourself.* When you do your part properly, give yourself a pat on the back. Remind yourself that you *are* doing a good job of parenting.

8

"I'd Do Anything for You, Dear"

In the musical *Oliver*, a child sings a song that goes, "I'd do anything for you, dear, *anything*...." That says something close to what we want to achieve with our children. Most people want children who *honor* their parents, *obey* them, *submit* to them gladly, and willingly do *anything* for them. And most of us want our children to do these things, not merely for money or candy or privileges, but for the love of their parents who would do anything for *them*.

Later, of course, such children will come to act on principles they have internalized and made their own.

Modeling, Teaching, and Social Reinforcement

How do you shape a child so that he loves and trusts you? How do you cause that miracle to happen? The most powerful tool for teaching love and trust is parent modeling. You must model love and trustworthiness for him. No matter how poor you are in the world's goods, no matter how broken up your family may be by the ravages of separation, divorce, disease, or death, you can be a model of love and reliability your children can count on. Do it. Besides modeling love and reliability, you can teach those things in words, explaining that you are what you are to them because you love them. Tell your child, in effect, "I'd do anything for you, Dear!" and back it up with deeds.

With your modeling and your teaching, combine social reinforcement for good behavior and achievement. We have already discussed social reinforcement, rewarding the child with your own positive reactions to his positive behavior.

Many parents seem to take the good for granted and give the child attention only when he's bad. So he learns to be bad if he wants his parents' notice. We can't tell you how many therapy clients we've heard tell the same story: "My parents hardly ever praised me, hardly ever noticed me, hardly ever told me I did well, hardly ever recognized it when I tried so hard to please them. All I can remember them doing was scolding me."

The Kind of People You Enjoy

Think about it. Picture someone you know who never reinforces others. You don't enjoy being with that person. You want to get away. Why? What is it that makes you wish you didn't have to be in his company? Carefully observe his behavior toward you. Such people almost *never* express genuine appreciation, approval, interest in you, attention or affection. You may feel they hardly notice you except insofar as you might constitute an audience. Instead, they focus on themselves, demand and expect special treatment, criticize, complain, and put you down. And they hardly ever show enthusiasm for anything, particularly anything you do, say, or care about.

Now think of the persons whose company you most enjoy. What do they do? Smile, let you feel their approval, show interest in you and what you are doing or what you have to say, share themselves with you but don't demand you attend only to them, praise you or compliment you, and demonstrate that they enjoy you. These people show enthusiasm with their interest. They are reinforcing people because they give you plenty of social reinforcement. It's easy to love them, easy to think, "I'd do anything for you."

Here is a sampling of social reinforcers:

- *Praise:* "Joey, your math paper is one of the neatest I've ever seen, and it's easy to read, too. Great job!"
- *Thanks:* "Janice, I really appreciate your dusting the dining room table and chairs for me. Thanks for giving me so much help!"
- *Applause:* "Hurray for you, Margie! I can't believe how you made the glasses shine when you dried them for me!"
- *Pleasure:* "Dana, you did all my yard work for me today. You make me feel so good when you show me so much love! You just made my day, honey!"
- *Bragging:* Telling others about the child's accomplishments. "You'll never believe what happened today. I got three compliments on how beautiful and new my car looked because Peter here did such a tremendous job of washing and waxing it for me. One guy even wanted to buy it. Did I feel special!"
- *Attention and approval:* "Jake, I've heard you can jump off the diving board and swim to the ladder all by yourself! That's so exciting! I want to see you do it. Will you please show me how you do it?" Or, when the child is busy, staying out of trouble, behaving beautifully, sit down on the floor beside her and say, "Molly, let me look at your building. Why, you're making something really special with those blocks. Do you need any help?"
- *Smile:* Mom, Dad, nothing in the world is so beautiful to a child as your smile. Let him see it often *when he is good*.
- *Loving touches:* Physical affection expressed in connection with the child's accomplishments or good behavior can become one of the most rewarding of all experiences. Many children are starving not only for parental attention but also for parental affection. Don't be afraid to touch your child! Fathers, take special note.

Don't Ignore Positive Omissions

When you're considering social reinforcement, remember to reinforce the child when she has not performed one of her undesirable behaviors for a reasonable time. Again, many parents ignore their kids when they omit performing a bad behavior. When Molly played with her baby brother without that painful squeeze she'd been giving him, her mother and father noticed and praised her for not hurting Eric.

As the child matures, the forms of social reinforcement must be progressively and carefully revised. Attention and recognition must be appropriate for the child's level of maturity and interests. Do appropriate things: When the child is older, go to his ball games, her track meets, his school plays, her choral concerts, enjoy them and convey your interest. And don't expect your young teen to show pleasure in your responses. She may appear to brush off your approval. But don't be misled by the front she puts up. Your attention and interest are still important.

Some Parents Object

One of the most common objections raised by parents to our plan for empowering them is their strange belief that it's inappropriate to reward people for doing right. They think other people should do right without getting cookies for it. Some protest, "I don't like the idea of *paying* my child for obeying me!"

Those who call reinforcement "bribery" are going much too far. A *bribe* is correctly distinguished from a legitimate reward by the fact that a *bribe* is given to influence a person in a position of trust, such as a judge. It's immoral and illegal for a judge to take bribes. It is not wrong for a judge to receive a reward for his work in the form of salary.

Those who object do have one point, even if their terminology isn't entirely valid. We *certainly* want our children to learn to do what's right just because it's right. But there's nothing wrong with learning how to do so with a system of incentives. Yes, it is unwise to train children to *always expect* some material reward for every good act. But reinforcement does form good behavior habits, and eventually the "external props"—that is, the tangible rewards— can be removed altogether.

Another question often raised touches on an issue we discussed earlier. As Roberta asked when we were planning her program, "Doesn't this make my love to my daughter *conditional*? If I give my child all these positive expressions only when she's good, won't she think she has to perform to win love?"

"Roberta," Candy responded, "I wondered about that at first, too. But I've come to realize that none of this makes my love conditional. I love our kids even when I'm punishing them—maybe especially then. The fact is, I need extra love to be willing to suffer with them when I'm punishing them. No, it's not my love that's conditional; it's the *way my love is expressed* that depends on the child's behavior. Isn't this precisely the way God tells us He treats His children? He loves them even when they sin,[1] but He also chastises or punishes them as a part of that very same love.[2]

Normal People Strive for Social Reinforcement

Furthermore, many of the rewards for which a normal, mature person strives are social, not tangible. Even in small things social reinforcers keep people going. For instance, watch two people chatting. See how they reinforce each other with *social* reinforcers, such as nods, smiles, interest, questions, sharing of information, praise, commendation. How long would the conversation continue if neither person rewarded the other by giving such signs of positive attention? Social reinforcement is the way most of our moral, spiritual and social behavior is acquired.

And social reinforcement is much more desirable in a

---

[1]"God shows his love for us in that while we were yet sinners Christ died for us" (Romans 5:8).

[2]"My son, do not regard lightly the discipline of the Lord, nor lose courage when you are punished by him. For the Lord disciplines him whom he loves" (Hebrews 12:6).

society where most people have plenty to eat. Not once have we ever heard a client say, "I didn't get enough cookies, candy, or TV time when I was growing up." But we have often shared the pain of clients who confided, "I didn't get enough attention [or approval or love] from my father or mother." Pastors seldom hear people complain or quit the church because nobody has paid them money for their services to the congregation, but most of them live in fear that they will inadvertently forget to recognize and give attention to someone who believes he deserves it.

Learning to Value Social Rewards

Children may need to learn to be truly reinforced by social rewards. At first, social reinforcers alone may not bring about the desired behavior change, especially if the child hasn't come to value them.

Because the child is not a cat or a dog, but a *person*, a valuable, eternal individual, because we're not just doing animal training, we want to emphasize love expressed through social rewards. That is why we recommend that even though, in many instances, you begin with tangible reinforcers, you remember to *pair them* with social reinforcers.

This coupling of social rewards with tangible rewards can be expected to cause the child increasingly to value social rewards alone. Because events that are coupled with something very reinforcing will themselves become more and more reinforcing.

In other words, if your smiles don't powerfully reward your child now, let him see you smile when you give him good food, candy, cookies and special treats. Let him see this blending of your smile with rewards often enough, and the smile will eventually come to mean much. In fact, it will itself become a powerful reward or reinforcer. This is why we've been urging you to remember always to give social reinforcers *along with tangibles*, for by so doing, you will eventually be able to drop most of the tangibles and rely on social rewards in your relationships with your children.

Do it something like this:

- "Jonathan, you made such fast, neat work of mowing that lawn, I'm really pleased. I'd like to do something for you. How about a treat at Dairy Queen tonight?" Keep your tone enthusiastic and positive.
- "Luann, you get a great big point on your chart for obeying me just now. You didn't argue even a little bit, you didn't complain, didn't even make a face, even though I dragged you away from what you were doing. And you did what I asked right away. I'm so impressed I'm gonna put this point up with a big red pen." Don't forget to smile and sound upbeat.

Social rewards are the "I'd do anything for you" makers. If you have to choose one lesson out of this book (you don't, you can learn them all), learn to give your children social reinforcement.

Review these points:

- For the *child*, parents must model such things as *love* and *trust*. Show your child an example of rewarding behavior.
- Give praise, attention, and recognition for good behavior, including the omission of objectionable deeds. Don't just fuss over bad behavior.
- Use physical affection as well as positive words and smiles, and pair tangible rewards with these social reinforcers.

9

Unintentional Reinforcement

We have discussed the ways in which you can begin to deliberately reinforce your child for the good conduct you want.

There is also a phase in which parents may need to *unlearn* poor child-training habits. It is very important to review the way training has occurred in your home and, without taking on the weight of guilt, see what can be changed. You might begin this by asking yourself, "What kinds of conduct might I be reinforcing without realizing it? Could it be that some of Susan's less desirable habits have been shaped by me all unawares? Might Luke's annoying traits be, in part, a result of my reinforcing him for them, when I didn't realize what I was doing?"

Let's look at some examples of how this unfortunate transaction takes place.

Maria—Trained to Ignore

Candy's heart went out to Maria. From observing her mother's constant nagging in our waiting room, Candy knew before the consultation that Maria was a noncompliant child. Compliant behavior means that the child learns to do what is asked without arguing, complaining, or stalling. Maria usually ended up doing what her mother asked, but only after all sorts of lackadaisical noncompliance, during which time she would get scads of attention from her nagging mother.

Occasionally, she did what she was asked to do immediately and without argument. This may seem contradictory, but almost all children are occasionally quite obedient all on their own. However, in Maria's case when she did comply, *nothing* happened. Her mother, Norma, systematically ignored Maria's good behavior! We saw the problem even before Maria's mother described it. Candy verified all this by asking Norma to collect data for one week regarding what she did when Maria complied and when she didn't. This child was *ignored* for obeying, and *reinforced* for disobeying. Norma was actually misapplying her parent power to accomplish the opposite of what she wanted.

How unfortunate, for many children, that attention from parents cannot be won by obedience. They have to *dis*obey to get their parents to notice them and speak to them.

The Interrupter

A friend and her little daughter visited us. The woman was trying to tell us about her trip to England. Tune in:

"... And then, we visited the British Museum. I wish I could take you there! What a wonderful—"

"MOMMY! MOMMY! MOMMY!"

"What is it, dear?"

"Mommy, I want to color in my coloring book."

"All right, dear, go ahead. Now, let me see, where was I—Oh yes, the British Museum. Well, anyway we saw a—"

"I can't find my green crayon, Mommy. Did you bring it?"

"Of course, dear, it's got to be in the box. Look for it. There's nothing like this particular museum anywhere. We saw Bible manuscripts that—"

"*It's not there!* You help me find it!"

As you can guess, if you've tried to carry on similar conversations with repeatedly interrupted parents, this pattern continued throughout the visit. Judy broke in, frequently, loudly, turning Shirley's narrative into a melange of broken sentences.

Rewarding Judy for Breaking In

Not only does Shirley *allow* Judy to interrupt others, she actually *rewards* Judy every time she breaks in. She does so by giving Judy *attention* and even *positive strokes* consistently and immediately after Judy intrudes on others' conversations. Don't miss another important observation. Judy reinforces Shirley for giving her attention by resuming her activities and leaving Shirley alone—briefly. In that way, Shirley is rewarded for giving Judy reinforcing attention.

You've seen it in others. You've wondered why such parents put up with constant interruption. But have you noticed the parent who thinks he's discouraging his child's repeated intrusions?

Perhaps you know someone whose child interrupts constantly when others are talking. And perhaps your friend doesn't reward his child *every* time he interrupts, but on the contrary ignores the kid's first, second, maybe even his third try. Meanwhile, the youngster interrupts more loudly, sounding more imperious each time. At last, exasperated, the parent responds loudly, "For cryin' out loud, stop interrupting! What *do* you want? All right, go ahead and have another caramel. But this time I mean it—it's positively the last one!"

This parent is creating an even bigger problem for himself. He is reinforcing his child with great emotional energy—a powerful measure of attention—and doing it intermittently. You will recall that *intermittent* reinforcement (rewarding only every so often, randomly) builds the strongest behavior habits. Tough habits to break! And, of course, Norman is rewarding Mark the way Maria and Judy rewarded their mothers—with brief respites following Mark's exasperated outbursts. So this parent, too, is developing a strongly reinforced habit of responding to interruptions.

What You Don't See

The "kicker" is that this parent, like the two mothers we've observed, doesn't even know he's *creating* a problem.

To investigate the effectiveness of this kind of unintentional reinforcement, experimenters asked the help of some classroom teachers. Before beginning the experiment, the researchers spent a great deal of time carefully observing the room, tallying the amount of time students spent out of their seats and the number of students typically not in their seats.

The teachers agreed that they would make a point of noticing whenever a pupil left his seat. Thereupon the teacher would call the child by name and tell him to take his seat. The experimenters noted that the children always returned to their seats when asked to. Strikingly, however, they found that the total time spent out of their seats by the children increased dramatically.

Why? The teacher was rewarding them with attention for being away from their own places. And the children rewarded the teachers by returning promptly to their places when asked. The teachers' habitual prompting was equally reinforced by the children's prompt obedience— which nearly always terminated very soon as the pupils left their chairs again to initiate the same cycle.

The Double-Reward System

Consider these examples, and you'll see the unintentional reinforcement teachers and parents give children, and also the unintentional reinforcement given back by the children. It's very important that you understand how this two-way pattern of unintentional rewarding builds strong unwanted habits into the adult-child interaction.

Tyler, believing he was out of the teacher's sight behind

the girl in front of him, emitted a sharp whistle. The teacher was not fooled. She reprimanded him sternly. As soon as she turned her back, Tyler turned toward the class and put on his cross-eyed face. The appreciative audience roared. And Tyler's clowning was greatly rewarded, both by the teacher's attention and by the amused responses of his fellow pupils. Will similar episodes occur again? What do you think?

Ginger's mother had a talk with her after she stayed out late one night, explained to her why she must be in the house by curfew time, what made her lateness a problem for Mom, how much she loved Ginger, and how reasonable it was for her to be worried about her late daughter. Ginger did not improve in her observance of the curfew, so her mother repeated her reasoning with the girl. Ginger stayed out late even more often. Is there a connection?

When our children were young, Debbie, the littlest, would try valiantly to participate in the dinner table conversation. Her brother, Martin, his mind riveted on his own interests, loudly interrupted, easily overriding Deb's soft small voice. Bill, touched by Debbie's tears, would silence Martin, permitting Debbie to talk. But Debbie cried again the very next evening at dinner when Martin interrupted her. Why? Bill had inadvertently rewarded her for crying when she would have done better to learn to say to Martin, "Please don't interrupt me, Martin. I'm not finished yet."

Ellen, in the kitchen, heard the TV on in the den. She knew Jerry had not yet gotten to his homework. "Jerry, what about your homework?" she called out.

"I'll do it, don't worry," growled the twelve-year-old, knowing he'd just purchased a few more minutes' peace.

Five minutes later, Ellen's prompt was more menacing. Again, Jerry put her off. At last, Ellen came to the den, framed the speech Jerry knew very well always meant the end of his rope was at hand. Grumbling, wearing his darkest, most threatening expression, Jerry switched off the TV and slammed his books onto the table. Ellen left the room frustrated but silenced.

What to Look For

Habitual prompting around home is generally called "nagging." Could unintentional reinforcement patterns similar to the ones we've described be the underlying cause of so much parental nagging?

Open your eyes to your own patterns of unintentional reinforcement. And, while you're at it, ask yourself how your child could be reinforcing you in ways neither of you intends, thus developing interaction patterns neither of you wants?

Be alert. Look for stubborn behavior that in spite of your efforts doesn't go away and may even be increasing. Do you reinforce it?

Look for patterns where your children eventually do what you tell them to do, but only after much prompting, explaining, nagging, or downright ugliness on your part.

Look for patterns where the behavior you want occurs only after you threaten the child with punishment of some kind.

Maybe you've recognized some of these patterns as you've read this chapter, and perhaps you'd like to think about how to eliminate them from your parent-child interactions.

Rules

Here are some general rules to apply to your specific case:

1. *Stop reinforcing behavior you don't want.* This will not be easy. You'll have to think about it carefully and plan a way to catch yourself. Perhaps another person can help you by calling your inadvertent reinforcements to your attention. Perhaps you can help yourself by starting a journal or a log book in which you keep track of every episode where you've caught yourself rewarding what you didn't want to reward. Write out the episode, what you did wrong, and what you plan to do instead next time the unwanted behavior occurs.

2. *Remember that attention is rewarding, even if it is negative attention.* So "lecturing" or "explaining why" or even yelling or "bawling out" the child *right after an unwanted action* will probably work just the opposite of the way you hope. It will probably *strengthen* the behavior.

Instead of giving attention after the behavior, select a completely different occasion. Sit down with the child and say something like, "I need to talk with you about a problem I'm having. It bothers me greatly when you interrupt me. If I'm chatting with another person, I want you to wait until we are finished, or until I speak to you, even if it is a long wait, before you speak to me. Do not interrupt me. If you do it again, I won't let you watch TV that day; and every time you do it after that, you'll have to give up a half hour of your favorite TV shows. For my part, when you and I are with someone else and I'm talking with that person, I'll make sure to stop and give you a chance to ask questions when I'm ready to do so. You are to wait until then." Carry out the program.

3. *If possible, ignore the unwanted behavior, especially if you've been reinforcing it.* If that isn't possible, *punish* the unwanted behavior without threatening first. Punishment can be mild, like time out, or more painful like removal of privileges. If nothing else, remove the child from the situation.

For example, the child asks for something to eat and you refuse, saying it's too near to a mealtime. The child whines. You pay no attention and go on about your business. When the whining intensifies, ignore it or leave the room. Do not respond to anything until after the child stops begging and whining.

If it's not possible to ignore the nagging and whining because guests are present or for some other reason, send the child to time out after the second request when you have firmly denied the first one. Return the child to "time out" every time he whines. (We will discuss how to use "time out" later.) If time out is not possible, take away TV time or another privilege. Remind yourself that you *must* carry out the deprivation of privileges after you assure the child he has lost them.

4. *Try reinforcing the child for alternative and incompatible behaviors.*

For example: "You didn't interrupt me once while we were visiting Mr. Smith. I'm so proud of you, and I'm going to buy you your favorite treat."

Or: "You didn't squirm around or leave your seat at all while we were at church. I was thinking to myself how great that was—I thought about it so much I could hardly listen to the sermon. I'm very pleased. I'd like to read you a special story to show you how happy you made me today."

Remember, your goal is to reinforce your child only for good behavior. So you want very much to discover any inadvertent reinforcement of the conduct you're trying to change.

Start examining your interactions with your child to discover your own heretofore unnoticed and unintended reinforcement of unwanted behavior. Remember:

- Parents can sometimes be the major cause of certain unwanted behaviors like interrupting, staying out late, waiting too long to respond when you call and others.
- Giving the child attention, even negative attention, by responding to requests, nagging, and explaining your reasons repeatedly may be very reinforcing to a child, especially if the child gets little attention for being good.
- Parental habits of inadvertent reinforcement can become quite strong because children reinforce their parents for giving them attention, even negative attention, and other reinforcers. You can monitor your own interactions with your child or ask someone else to help you to discover and alter habits of inadvertent reinforcement.

10

Using Punishment Effectively

"Anyone who whines will have to go into the house for a while," said Bill matter-of-factly. On this sunny day, two of our grandchildren, Jenny, age five, and Jacob, three, had come over for a swim. Jacob had recently discovered the unpleasant habit of whining and pouting when he found things were not going his way. On this day, nobody had whined, so it was a perfect time to make the contingency crystal clear. Before too long, however, Jacob complained. "It's my turn to have the inner tube. Jenny's had it too long!" And he began to whine and pout.

"Jacob, go into the house and wait until we call you," Bill said, refusing to yield to Jacob's sobs. After a few minutes in the house, Jacob, at our invitation, came out to the pool smiling. This time, he was clearly determined to communicate in more acceptable ways when he was frustrated by his big sister. Once, just a week or so later, Jacob had to be sent into the house for whining. After that, we haven't once had occasion to send him inside. There was no more whining at poolside.

Punishment Works

Punishment effectively changes behavior. And if administered properly, it does so very rapidly indeed.

Unfortunately, punishment has these days acquired a bad name. With a few—a *very* few—"experts" and a good many more confused parents, punishing children is out. A small minority of books for parents give the impression that punishing a child somehow violates his rights. Some parents simply won't tolerate the pain they themselves feel when it's necessary to deprive a child of a privilege or impose an unpleasant experience on her. They feel so bad they take what they believe to be an easy way out like threatening or yelling at the child.

Maybe you've allowed somebody to convince you that if you punish your child, you're not showing him unconditional love.

If you're one of those frightened parents who, one way or another, has come to avoid punishment in favor of empty threats, constant nagging, or simply tolerating bad behavior, you ought to consider very carefully the value of punishment *for the sake of the child*. And when you come right down to it, doesn't it take far more love to punish a child appropriately than to avoid dealing with his behavior?

What Is Punishment?

You might have your doubts about punishment partly because you haven't really ever taken the time to understand what punishment is. Many people view punishment as retribution, a kind of "getting even" with the child so that "justice" is done and he "gets what he deserves." While such ideas may have a legitimate place in the penal system and the criminal justice system, they have nothing whatever to do with the use of punishment for children. In our context, punishment has one purpose: not getting back at the child, not venting your anger at him, not making him pay, but *training*. Punishment is a tool for changing behavior in the *training* of a child. We hope to change the way you view punishment. Stop thinking, "He deserves X" and start telling yourself instead, "X is what he needs right now to help him change his behavior."

Let's take an unemotional look at the truth about punishment. As we are using the term, punishment means any event which, following immediately after a behavior, reduces the probability of the behavior occurring again.

Carefully study the definition of punishment. You can properly refer to something as punishment if *it occurs after the child does what he shouldn't and if its effect is to reduce the child's inclination to repeat the undesirable action.*

Notice that punishment is not defined as awful, terrible, excruciating, or in any way painful. In the above definition, there is not a single suggestion that an event must cause pain in order to be considered punishment. You are probably surprised that punishment need not hurt. We emphasize it because many people think punishment must be cruelly painful. Some readers may not think some procedures we suggest are painful enough to really punish.

But the aim is *not* to hurt children. It's to train them. Remember, if an event weakens behavior, it's punishment, whether it hurts much or not. And no matter how much you may think it hurts, an event can't be considered punishment *if it does not work to cause the behavior to diminish in frequency and/or intensity.*

Punish Immediately

Be aware, too, that *if punishment occurs too long after the unwanted behavior, it won't have any effect.* Does that help you to understand one reason why the American criminal justice system has little or no remedial effect on criminal behavior? For the very same reason, a parent who punishes a child at Christmastime by denying a much-wanted gift for a transgression that occurred in August is creating needless distress to no effect. It may hurt the child, but it's not punishment because it occurs too long after the unwanted behavior to have any effect.

Always Use Rewards

Remember as well that *although punishment effectively suppresses unwanted behavior, it does not eradicate the behavior.* You may cause a child to stop doing something through punishment, but the suppressed behavior can always return later on. That is why it's important to use positive reinforcement—especially lots of social reinforcement—to strengthen the desire of the child *not to perform* the unwanted action. When the child manages to perform according to your wishes, and to omit the bad behavior, *notice the effort made and reward it.*

> *Example:* You haven't spilled anything on yourself during this whole meal. I'm so pleased. Now I won't have to wash and iron your clothes so soon. What a break for me! Thanks for being so careful.

> *Example:* I've noticed something wonderful. You two haven't fought with each other once today. That's so enjoyable for me. It's been a real pleasure to have you two come with me to the toy store. And you know what? I'd like to get you each something you'd really like to show how good I feel about the way you've treated each other.

If It Doesn't Work, It Isn't Punishment

A final important point: *Punishment isn't punishment if it has no effect at all on the tendency of the child to repeat his bad behavior.* If you're doing something about your child's infractions and it has no effect, it isn't punishment, even if it's unpleasant for the child. Sometimes parents complain that they "punish" their child, but he keeps right on breaking the rules. What we do next is try to determine why results are so discouraging. And most often we find that the "punishment" probably isn't true punishment.

For instance, many parents give children the order: "Go to your room." Of course, children's situations vary, as do children themselves. Some may find time in their rooms punishing. But some children don't. Their parents don't stop to think that the child's room is the one place in the house where all the tangible rewards they've ever bought for him are kept. There in his room are his toys, his train, his computer, his books, his tapes and his stereo. How much "punishment" effect can you expect this cache of positive reinforcers to exert? We've already pointed out the fallacy involved when you think that "having a talk with her" after an infraction is sufficiently punishing when in reality it may be nothing but reinforcing attention. Most children are not in fact punished by the scoldings, cross words, threats, dire predictions, complaints, or even the light slaps many parents believe ought to be effective. If what you're doing isn't working, do something else.

Punishment, like reinforcement, must be applied contingently, immediately, and consistently—every time the target action occurs.

Some Sample Punishments

Time out is effective for young children of about ages three to eight, but may be less so for older youngsters and adolescents. First, choose a place where the child will go for time out—a place (not her room) where there are no obvious positive reinforcers. A spare bedroom, an empty walk-in closet, or a bathroom work very well. Next, explain to the child that there will be times when you will tell her "Go to time out." At that point, you will expect her to stop whatever she is doing and go straight to whatever place you choose, and sit quietly until the kitchen timer beeps or rings. You will set the timer for three minutes and when the child hears the timer, she can come out and resume play. We recommend that you even have a rehearsal, and explain that if there is a fuss, you'll set the timer for an additional three minutes. Use this procedure for one specific behavior you are trying to suppress and use it consistently and immediately. Do *not* use time out for an all-purpose response to anything you don't like. It's best reserved for one or two behaviors. Then when they have been learned well, it can be used for another one or two.

Overuse of time out can render it less effective. Remember that the full name of this procedure is *"time out from reinforcement,"* because it works, not by causing pain but by removing the child from ongoing reinforcement derived from her play.

Response cost. With this procedure, you deprive the child of something valuable to him like the use of a toy, a bike, a stereo or television. Or you may deprive him of an expected or routine treat. Monetary fine, suspension of driving privileges, restrictions on freedom, removal of telephone rights are all examples. If you are using a chart, tokens, stars, or similar exchangeables, you can remove tokens as a punisher.

Spanking. We will discuss physical punishment in a separate chapter.

Remember:

- Punishment is an event that weakens behavior, and if it doesn't "work" it isn't punishment, no matter now unpleasant it may be. If it "works" it is punishment even if it isn't horrendously painful.
- Punishment should be administered consistently, not haphazardly, and it should occur as soon as possible after the unwanted behavior occurs.
- Punishment may be time out, a monetary fine, removal of privileges, restrictions on freedom, or depriving the child of the use of a toy.

11

Physical Punishment: Yes or No?

Suppose your nine-year-old boy has been especially trying all day long. He repeatedly teased his sister in the back
seat of the car. He sneaked treats for himself, and complained about every request you made. And now he's whining because you want to watch the news and he wants to
watch cartoons. Then he yells at you—and finally you lose
it!

Now you're furious! You're sure you've put up with more
than the human parental constitution was made to tolerate.
You feel like slugging him right in the mouth. You wonder
if you ought to spank him. Should you? Wouldn't it "do him
good" for a change? Or "teach him a lesson"?

Let's imagine you have a toddler, age two, who has been
warned about playing in the street in front of your house.
You look out the window only to find that Lisa has opened
the backyard gate somehow and, unmindful of her drooping
wet diaper, is collecting pebbles from the gutter as automobiles whiz by a few feet away. You nearly jump out of
your skin, run for the front door, and snatch your precious
little girl out of harm's way. You think you ought to spank

her—and at the same time tell her emphatically she must stop going off the curb into the street. Would this be a good way to handle the situation?

Try this one. Your eight-year-old son has developed the habit of lying to you. You have frequently, but not always, been able to verify that he has deliberately told you an untruth to avoid punishment. You have tried using response cost by deducting a monetary fine from his allowance when you've caught him lying. You decide the only thing left to do is to spank him every time you catch him telling you an untruth. Is this a good idea?

Consider the Place of Spanking

If many modern parents find themselves shoved into a no-win conflict over the issue of when and whether to punish their children at all, many more have read or heard that no child should ever be spanked. Some media persons unaccountably equate any corporal punishment with child abuse. There are people who would like to have parents investigated and punished by the state for using physical punishment. Are these people correct when they make no distinction between child abuse and corporal punishment?

Not at all. We have found spanking—especially if used rarely, and if administered properly—to be very effective punishment. We have also found that such corporal punishment does absolutely no harm.

We urge parents to consider the use of spanking as an effective behavior-change tactic, and to reserve spanking for very special situations. We urge you to spank your child occasionally, because very wise people have, for centuries, counseled that corporal punishment has a place in child rearing. The wisdom literature of the Bible even suggests that parents who don't use spanking at all may lack love. (See Proverbs 13:24.)

Speaking behaviorally, spanking that is not abused or overused can be a very effective punishment, quickly suppressing the behavior for which it is applied.

Be Aware of the Costs

There are certain costs connected with the use of physical punishment. You should know what they are and be prepared to pay them if necessary. They should also cause you to limit your use of spanking to situations calling for immediate behavior change and unambiguous powerful punishment. For example, the two-year-old who keeps running into a dangerous street can learn very quickly if he's caught in the act and punished with a few sharp, stinging swats on the bottom. One situation where spanking can seem inconvenient is in public. In such cases, though it may be a bother to you, you should spank when necessary though not "in public." If possible, take the child to a bathroom or a corner where no one is watching. Never make a spectacle of punishment.

We have stated that there are drawbacks to the use of physical punishment. Here are some of the findings of psychologists about the negative effects of inflicting physical pain on children:

- *It causes anger and resentment.* No reason to be surprised at this. A part of the instinctive response of the human being to being hurt is anger. We don't want to be the focus of our own children's rancor. And we assume you too suffer pain when you feel required to do something to incur your children's displeasure. But it's not the end of the world if they're upset with us. They'll get over it. So will we. Meantime, if our love is for real, we'll be willing to tolerate their temporary rejection to secure their training in right behavior.
- *It pairs the person administering the spanking with unpleasantness.* By this time you know about classical conditioning: So you understand that if Dad or Mom practically never interacts with little Erica except to spank her, that person will likely become a negative presence for Erica! She may then fear and avoid the punisher. We can't say it often enough, so let us repeat it again: Catch the child when she's being good and give her abundant loving positive reinforcement at those times. If you do

that, an occasional spanking won't destroy your relationship with her.

- *It models aggressive behavior for the child.* Remember, you are a model for your child. Especially if Johnny gets the impression that you are reinforced in some way for spanking, he may learn to hit others when they do something to offend him. One reason for *never striking a child on an angry impulse, never punching him or hitting him* is to avoid modeling physical aggression in anger. To lessen the negative modeling effects, do not swat your child as an act of annoyance, do not hit him in a spate of fury, do not strike him willy-nilly, and do not use physical punishment often. When you spank, spank him on the bottom.

- *It may cause an increase in the behavior you're trying to punish.* Those parents who do not shower generous quantities of heartfelt positive feedback on their offspring probably ought never to spank. That is because the only attention the little ones receive occurs during physical punishment. Spanking may actually be reinforcing for the child because he is so deprived of any other parental attention. This effect might be even more pronounced if the parent administers rather innocuous light swats that cause no pain. If most of your interactions with your child involve swatting him, you might actually be creating a badly behaved youngster!

Discriminate Hitting *From* Spanking

Nothing in this chapter should be construed as an endorsement of hitting. We have read some advice columns for parents written by people who seem unable to discriminate between spanking and hitting. And we suppose there are parents, some of whom may pick up this book, who are incapable of making that discrimination as well. We can and do make such a discrimination and we consider the discrimination extremely important.

By *hitting*, we mean the violent belting of children by parents who have not learned to control their own behavior.

Whacking your child because you are irritated by his actions, slugging him whenever you feel an impulse to attack, and telling yourself your child drives you to beating him not only signals very poor parenting, but it also sounds an alarm.

If you habitually hit your child, *pay attention to this warning signal*. It means you need help. Before it's too late, consult a competent professional and follow that person's advice. You'll feel much better about your relationship with your children, and with yourself.

When Might You Spank?

When *should* you spank? We believe spanking ought to be reserved and not resorted to willy-nilly nor chosen as the only punishment you impose because it's easy to do, and it doesn't require much creative thought.

A very big problem occurs when you use spanking as the only form of punishment. Many times the child has done something you wish to discourage, but it's not so serious you're willing to inflict physical pain on him for it. So, as a result, though punishment is definitely needed and warranted, you don't do anything because it's not "bad enough."

We can't tell you in detail each situation in which you should spank. We would, however, suggest you reserve spanking for the following three kinds of situations. We're not saying you must spank then, but we're suggesting that these may be opportune times to consider using spanking:

- When the young child will not stay out of a particularly dangerous situation and you can't safely delay making a deep impression on him.
- When you're in a place where other kinds of punishment are not very readily available and the child, aware of this, believes he can defy you.
- When dealing with a behavior that has apparently not been affected by other kinds of punishment but which must be stopped for the child's own good.

Advice on How to Spank

We can't resist giving you some detailed advice about how to spank. Let's assume you are resorting to spanking only rarely, that you give positive reinforcement galore, and that when punishment is necessary you ordinarily use some of the nonphysical methods described in the last chapter. But sometimes you feel that spanking makes lots of sense. Here's how we suggest you do it.

First, get yourself under control. Talk to yourself. "Cool it. Just calm down. She's getting to you because you're tired, and when she does this it makes you feel like a failure." Tell yourself the truth. "She's not trying to make you feel like a zero. But she needs to learn quickly not to do that behavior. So calm down. That's it. Now you can handle the situation in a way you won't regret later."

Don't wait too long to administer the spanking. Remember, punishment should follow very quickly after a behavior. If you wait too long, the spanking will lose its effectiveness. If you can't calm down rather quickly to the point where you're not going to batter your child, then use some other form of punishment. Don't wait for half a day to administer a spanking. Don't promise that when the other parent gets home, the spanking will be administered by him.

Spank so that it hurts, but never cause injury. If you're going to spank her, don't make it a gentle love tap. Unless the spanking hurts, it might even reinforce and strengthen her bad behavior. Don't bruise her either. *Never strike out so as to hit a child around the face or head. Take the time to position her so the spanking will be administered on the bottom.*

Tell the child why he or she is being punished. Say, "I'm spanking you so you will stop going into the street. You must not go into the street unless a big person is with you." / "I'm spanking you so you will stop lying to me." / "I'm spanking you so you will find it painful to disobey me. I want you to do as I ask you to without complaining or putting it off." Do not say, "This hurts me more than it hurts you." If that's true, then the spanking is not what it ought to be. It should hurt the child more than it hurts you, and it should make you feel that you have acted appropriately.

Should you give your child physical love and reassurance immediately following a spanking? We don't know of any research on this issue, but in most situations, with most children, we don't think so. We are aware that some people do advise this. But it appears to us that you might confuse the issue by immediately administering positive reinforcement when you are trying to punish. What are you rewarding the child for? At this time, the point is punishment. By gathering the child up in your arms and declaring your love and affection, you may actually reinforce the entire sequence of events that occurred previously: the misbehavior, and even getting the spanking. You should give the child plenty of love and lots of reinforcement—but at other times and in the context of *good* behavior. Give physical affection at the next occasion when that is your routine, for example, at bedtime.

Some parents wonder about spanking adolescents. Our advice is to stop spanking when your child reaches puberty, or shortly thereafter. We haven't been positively impressed by the results some parents have obtained by spanking older teens. They are beginning to move into adult behaviors and will respond better to deprivation of privileges and fines than to spanking. Your object in spanking is not to humiliate.

Use Positive Reinforcement

When you notice your child making efforts to change his behavior following a spanking, be sure to give huge quantities of positive reinforcement for the efforts at change. Don't wait until the change is perfect.

Always reward your child for progress, and for every effort he makes.

12

Ten Common Mistakes

Clinicians practicing psychotherapy quickly discover how many creative ways people can misconstrue counsel and advice. We have discovered that, like us, people try to do things right, and often get it wrong. And we've also found that, like us, they can learn from the mistakes of others.

We want to describe and illustrate ten common mistakes you can make in using parent power.

Ten Don'ts

Mistake #1: Waiting for big changes before delivering reinforcement.

Thirteen-year-old Terry was wild with enthusiasm—at first. Her parents had just read a book about reinforcement and they too were full of enthusiasm. What a deal: If she would bring her grade-point average up from a $C-$ to a B over this coming school year, they would let her fly to the West Coast to visit her friend Sally next summer!

Terry could hardly wait. She sat down to do homework as soon as she got home from school, went to extra trouble to double-check her work, and made certain she handed in her papers. After three weeks of this intense effort, Terry became ill with the flu and had to miss a week of school. When she returned, she felt completely out of it, because she didn't know what the teachers were talking about. It looked to her as if all her valiant efforts had been wasted.

Soon she went back to her former patterns of procrastination and indifference. What had begun as a challenging adventure had petered out by the end of the second month of classes. Her parents were disappointed, but that was not all. They blamed Terry for her "laziness" and decided that their child wouldn't change and using reinforcement wouldn't make any difference. Terry's self-image took a beating too.

What more could Terry's parents have done than make such a generous offer? What on earth would it take to inspire their daughter to perform well? Disgusted, Terry's father put it this way, "We can't give her the moon!"

Their mistake was a common one. They offered Terry what was for her a spectacular reward in exchange for several months of sustained effort. Rarely will such an offer fulfill parents' hopes, because *reinforcement that's delayed doesn't reinforce powerfully.* A good deal of experimental evidence has demonstrated that the optimal time interval between the performance of the child and the presentation of a reward is the shortest interval possible.

Terry's parents should have rewarded her *each night* for doing her homework, and *each day* for small improvements in the quality of her work. Furthermore, they should have rewarded her for *any* improvement rather than wait for her grades to reach a predetermined and unprecedentedly high level. They should have first rewarded Terry for simply putting in time and effort, regardless of the grades achieved; then, later, they should have begun placing contingencies on neatness, accuracy, and grades. When the steps required for reinforcement are too large, and reinforcement is not forthcoming for small increments in performance, the child will soon give up.

So it's a mistake to tell a C− student you'll give him a large reinforcer in ten months if he'll get all B's or A's. Don't wait for your child with D's to get an A, or for the sloppy one to clean her room like a professional maid, or for the novice to do a fault-free job of waxing the car, or for the little screamer to behave like a perfect gentleman when company comes. When you fail to reward the child for small steps, you will fail. If the steps are too large, and reinforcement too long delayed, the child will give up!

Mistake #2: Inserting "hornets" into your reinforcers.

Our youngest daughter, Debbie, put on her sweat suit one morning, expecting to feel rewarded with snug, comforting warmth. Instead, she felt a sharp pain in her hip. A hornet had hidden in the suit, and when she disturbed him, he stung her.

Some parents slip "hornets" into the reinforcers they give their children. How? By adding a "but" to their praises. Some people think only in terms of *yes-buts*: "Yes, it's a beautiful day, *but* the mosquitos have been horrid." "Yes, I do feel better, *but* I know the headache could easily come back." People who think in *yes-buts* are apt to insert hornets into the reinforcers they give their children. "You look nice, *but your socks don't match your shirt."* "It's nice you got up without being called, but *you didn't finish all your breakfast."* The result of this is a zero-sum. Add a *"but"* to praise or recognition and you have subtracted its reward value. You end up with zero, if not worse.

For instance, Alan has agreed to spend 30 minutes every day on his homework as a step toward improving his grades. Alan's father looks over his son's completed assignment and says, "You did put in the time—but this paper! Alan, it's a mess. It looks like a chicken walked over it with ink on its feet."

This father's sarcasm stings like a hornet, but he'll tell everybody he praised Alan for what he did right and he just can't understand why his son doesn't make progress in school. The hornets Alan's father added to his reinforcer punished Alan for trying; he didn't, in fact, reward him at all. There won't be much progress here.

At this initial stage, Alan's dad would have done well to

say, "You did it. You put in 30 minutes and you finished all your homework. You know, that really makes me feel good because I know it means progress. Nice going, son!" Later on, he can start requesting and reinforcing neater work.

Little Jodi, age six, offers to dry the dishes. Her offer is accepted and she does dry the dishes—sort of. Jodi's mother doesn't have to be a perfectionist to see that there will be water marks on the glasses. She begins redrying them in front of the little girl. "Thanks for doing dishes, Jodi, but you didn't get them dry enough. Look here—you left spots on the glasses and they'll dry streaked." What do you think will happen to Jodi's interest in helping her mother with the dishes?

If this mother had only said, "Look what a good job you did! I bet most six-year-olds couldn't dry dishes for their families. But you did it! You're getting to be such a big girl and I'm so pleased. Thanks!" Had she done so, she'd be putting "money in the bank" toward some day having a helpful little pair of hands around the house.

Mistake #3: Losing interest and becoming slipshod about reinforcement.

Joan put a chart for her daughter Penny on the refrigerator door, recording Penny's earned points on the chart with lots of praise and recognition *every time* Penny remembered to brush her teeth, take her shower, and wash her hair without prompting or procrastinating. Penny became almost perfectly self-grooming very quickly.

After a couple of weeks, Joan became accustomed to Penny's new level of responsibility for herself, and gradually lost her zeal. She would sometimes delay giving her daughter rewards. She might think it was just too far to run downstairs to the refrigerator door when she was upstairs making beds at the time Penny performed one of her duties. Sometimes she found herself watching a TV show when her daughter earned a point. "It's too much of an interruption right now to put up her points. I'll try to remember later," she told herself. Therefore, Penny sometimes didn't get her points at all, and other times the recording of them was delayed. Besides, Joan's initial enthusiasm faded as she now gave her daughter halfhearted "positive social reinforcement."

The effect of Joan's failure to carry out the program exactly as planned began to show. Penny's self-grooming slipped lower, even if it didn't quite reach its initial low level.

The single most common cause of failure of reinforcement programs in the home is the failure of parents to actually carry out the programs. Gerald Patterson and his associates, described in a previous chapter, demonstrated adequately that when a well-tailored reinforcement program sinks like an ocean liner splintered by an iceberg, the shipwreck is due to parents losing interest and so failing to work the program. We wish we could call every reader on the telephone every day to pump you up, but we can't: So you might want to give some careful thought to the question of *keeping yourself on board a watertight ship* before you start a program with your kids!

One device some parents have found effective is *contracting,* to give an additional reinforcer to the child who discovers a parental lapse and calls that parent's attention to it. This really gives the child the responsibility for keeping the parent on-target. Do you think it would help you?

Mistake #4: Giving the reinforcer before the target behavior occurs.

You read about Hal and Jan in Chapter 10—the parents who gave their son Scott the automobile he was to get for going to school *before* he completed the program. Perhaps very few parents would commit such a colossal blunder. But how often we've heard (and probably even said) things like: "Bobby, if you'll promise to eat all your dinner, I'll give you a cookie now. Otherwise you'll have to wait until after dinner." Of course Bobby promises because he *means* to eat all his dinner. But later, when the cookie has gone down sweetly and the dinner involves too many vegetables—will

Bobby perform according to his agreement? No way! The cookie should have been saved in a place where Bobby could see it, but not taste whenever he wished. Then, when the last bite of broccoli has disappeared, the cookie will be presented as a reinforcer.

Remember the proper order: the behavior, then the reward. Never: the reward, then the behavior.

Mistake #5: Using threats as behavior motivators.

"Colleen, if you don't get in this house immediately, you won't get the extra TV time you were promised for being prompt."

This approach may fool you. It may appear to work because the child develops an uncanny sense for when you really mean it and when you still have a few good threats left in you. That child will always wait until the threat is really serious before coming in.

Perhaps you've often found yourself wishing other parents whose children are climbing all over you on an airplane or stepping on your feet in the checkout line would *stop threatening and do something*. It's a pretty sad situation when a helpless parent delivers such a threatening line, and the child obviously has no intention whatever of listening.

When you next intend to threaten, skip the threat and go ahead and instigate the punishment. "I called you five minutes ago and you haven't come in yet. You may not watch your favorite TV show tonight. Come in now." If the child doesn't respond, say, "You still haven't come right away, as I asked you to. So you'll have to skip all your TV shows tonight. Come in now."

Maybe you object: "Junior is entitled to some warning, isn't he?" Why? Isn't he expected to obey you? Hasn't he ever heard that compliance with your requests is his duty? Of course he has. He has no more need of a warning than you need for an officer to tap you on the shoulder and warn you to be sure to stop at the next red light or else.

If you punish—even mildly, but definitely—at the point where you usually threaten, you will soon be able to delete threats from your interactions with your children.

Mistake #6: Giving away what you hope to sell.

A farmer got up early in the morning to pick fresh corn, drove to town, parked at a busy intersection, and proceeded to set up his stand. But nobody stopped to buy his lovely fresh sweet corn. Puzzled, the farmer finally drove back down the road to have a look around. Soon he spotted the problem. Traffic was piled up around another farmer who had set up a stand and, hoping to attract customers for his garden vegetables, was giving fresh corn to all comers free of charge. No way was the first farmer going to sell his corn until his "competitor" either boosted his price or ran out of product.

An elementary lesson in market economics, right? Yet parents who complain that their reinforcement program "doesn't work" have sometimes failed to apply this lesson: They continue to make the "reinforcer" available whenever the child wants it.

For instance, if you're using M&M's to reward your child for compliance, you mustn't have a dish of them sitting out where he can help himself whenever he wishes. If you want to make his TV time conditional on making his bed properly before breakfast, you can't let him have unrestricted access to the TV. If money is the reinforcer, you can't supply it whenever he comes to you with a heartrending story about how he wants to go to the ball game with his friends, but doesn't have the price of a ticket.

Remember, if you're puzzling over what to use as a reinforcer, notice what your child does when she is free to choose any activity. Does she call a friend for a chat? Does she read in her room? Does she watch TV? Does she ride her bike? Let's say she can't seem to get enough telephone socializing so you decide to give her 15 minutes' phone time whenever she sets the table for a meal. Fine. But don't forget to make clear that *all* telephone time must now be earned unless it's for some purpose other than socializing. Don't *weaken*. You can't let her use the telephone unless she has earned the time.

Steve's TV time was not restricted by his parents. Unfortunately, they allowed the thirteen-year-old to watch whatever he chose. The only limit put on Steve was that he could not preempt the TV when others in the family wanted to watch their favorite programs. You can guess what happened when his mother offered to let Steve earn more TV time as a reinforcer for sweeping the front walk. Nothing. Steve had no interest in carrying out the program.

Some children are granted almost total freedom, given unlimited money, and furnished with virtually everything they ask for. When you try to come up with reinforcers for changing their behavior, you may make the mistake of thoughtlessly using money, toys, and freedom that the child can get easily without carrying out the program. This doesn't work. You must either come up with something the child can't obtain easily anyway or put restrictions on the flow of things he has been accustomed to obtaining without effort.

Mistake #7: Using punishment when you could just as well use positive reinforcement.

Does the word "discipline"—which really means "training"—automatically suggest punishment to you? Just as some people are pessimistic in their interpretation and expectations of life and some look at the painful side of every situation, some parents seem to think mainly in terms of *punishment*. These are not people who judiciously use punishment when it is necessary to control their children's behavior. These are folks who seldom think of using rewards at all.

By now you know we advocate the use of punishment. But we don't want you to become a *punishing parent*—one who always resorts to deprivation, response cost, or pain. Some parents are so punishment-oriented their children's first association with their names is punishment. "My dad," they say, "is that fellow who comes home every once in a while to spank me."

Use punishment, but don't be a punishment-oriented parent.

Think first of using positive reinforcement. Can you teach your child this lesson using enthusiasm, praise and other rewarding consequences?

Very often, you can work with positive reinforcement rather than punishment by simply rewarding the child for *not doing* what you would punish him for doing. You may also combine both consequences—that is, punish him for doing the act, and reward him for a period of not doing it. Try to think of ways to substitute rewards for empowerment rather than punishers.

Mistake #8: Bestowing reinforcement grudgingly.

We've frequently met parents who seem stingy with reinforcers. They will tell us something like, "Well, yes, Tony did take the dog out for a walk—but it's his dog! I don't want to praise him for that. He *should* take care of his own dog. Why does he *deserve* praise for doing what he ought to do?" Or they'll say, "*What*—give her a dollar for making her bed? No way! It took her only five minutes. A quarter is more than enough pay for that amount of effort! I make the beds in this house for nothing. Why shouldn't she?"

We recall one couple who had started a successful program in their home. They weren't happy, though. Each of them said something like, "I can't feel good about giving these kids presents and money—or even all this praise and thanks. They shouldn't need rewards for helping out and doing right." Some say they just don't want to "pay" the child for doing what is, after all, only his duty, or they don't want to "spoil" the child with rewards. One group of such parents doesn't want to pay the child "too much" for doing "too little," and the other group doesn't want to reward the child at all. Both have a rigid attitude toward their kids, seeing them as little adults "in their employ," from whom they should get a day's work for a day's pay, rather than seeing them as learners they're training.

If you're one of those who worries about too much reinforcement, switch gears. You're not dealing with an employee who is getting more than he's giving; you're training and shaping a child's life! The truth is, you *want* to give the child lots of reinforcement. The more the better because when you're giving reinforces your program is working.

Don't be stingy. Be glad if what you are doing is working so well you're giving your child enormous amounts of recognition, approval, praise, money or other tangibles.

Mistake #9: Trying to change too many behaviors at one time.

Sometimes enthusiastic parents think of a large number of target behaviors they feel should be changed. Then they'll go to work on half a dozen or more change programs at one time. Soon they realize they can't remember, monitor, or reinforce the child for such an array of different target behaviors.

Others initiate ambitious programs with several children at once, learning only later how difficult it is to keep track of everything for everybody at the same time.

We have found that it's usually best to begin with one child and one behavior. If compliance (obedience executed immediately on command without arguing, complaining, or procrastinating) is a problem, it might make the rest of the work easier to begin with that. Then after the child obeys nine commands out of ten without arguing, complaining, or procrastinating, introduce another target behavior or maybe two others. Then, when those are going well, it might be time to bring another child along into his or her own training program. At any rate, it's usually best to introduce one target behavior to one child at a time. When you've learned from experience, expand as you find it comfortable to do so.

Incidentally, it isn't unusual for other children in a family to beg to be put on a program of reinforcement, because they see the first child receiving lots of reinforcement. So, don't be surprised if you discover this *"me too"* in your own brood. If your children are asking for the program, you have a superb opportunity to begin with a major advantage.

Mistake #10: Failing to define the target behaviors precisely.

Do you know for certain what you want your child to do? Have you ever taken the time to spell it out for yourself? Clarify, define, and write down what you want before you even begin: "Be sure to come in before dark"; "Clean your room"; "Obey me"; "Be polite." Look closely at those commonly given directives. What do they mean? All too often they mean whatever the *child* wants them to mean.

You may have told your child to come in before dark, believing you've made very clear that he is to come in while the sun is still visible in the sky—while he interprets that to mean he can slip in just as it's getting pitch dark. You may have said, "Clean your room," and think you have told your child to hang up all his clothes, make his bed, vacuum his rug, and dust his dresser and bedstead. He thinks he's cleaned his room if he picks up the junk on the floor and throws it into the closet, that he's made his bed if he pulls the covers up toward the pillows. Are you clear about the obedience you want? Or do you let the child argue and procrastinate and drive you nearly bananas before he finally does what you ask—and then call that obedience? And he can interpret politeness as he wishes. Who knows exactly what that means?

Think it out. What *do* you want? Then tell him. "Be in the house at your desk doing your homework by 7:15." "Make your bed by doing this...."

Before you begin a program, you may have to keep a written log of unsatisfactory interactions with your child and study it carefully. Then locate the behaviors you want to change and write out in detail what you want the child to learn to do differently. (More about this later.)

Don't make the mistake of not knowing exactly what you want to change and how!

There are lots of other possible mistakes. For example, giving all the attention and goodies to a problem child in order to keep him from erupting, while the good child goes unrewarded and unnoticed. Or getting so involved with changing behavior, charts, tokens and points you forget to have a *personal, loving relationship* with your child. Or persisting with a program that isn't working, rather than looking at the reasons why it isn't working and trying to make changes. If your program isn't working and you can't find your weak spots, it might well be worthwhile to consult with a trained psychologist. But we believe the ten mistakes we've described are the pitfalls you're most likely to slip into.

If you can keep from making these ten mistakes, you will still need to add one ingredient to the mix: your own *enthusiasm*! Give your child your best, whatever you do with him. And when you're giving reinforcement, working on a program of behavior change, you're doing something important and thrilling, which, in your best judgment, will add excellence to the child's life!

13

Starting a Point System

Now, you're ready to apply all you've learned. So we're going to help you get started with what is often called a *point system* or a *home token economy*. Perhaps you're still thinking, "I've tried that and it didn't work." We believe that if what we're going to describe doesn't work, the problem will be found somewhere in the execution of the program. You might have had faulty or incomplete instructions.[1]

Sam and Marian Bredemeier consulted us as a last resort. Like many adoptive parents, they had misgivings. Had they made a mistake when they took Clayton into their home? Would his genetic endowment thwart their every effort to be loving, effective parents? Five-year-old Clayton was, as Sam explained to us, "totally out of control."

"He defies us, makes us feel totally helpless, and doesn't do anything we want him to do," Sam said through tight

---

[1]We have made much use of the research of Gerald Patterson and his associates. We bring it to you with confidence that research results and our own experience have consistently testified that it works. If you would like to read some of Patterson's work, here are a couple of references: Gerald R. Patterson, *Families: Applications of Social Learning to Family Life*, revised (Champaign, Ill.: Research Press, 1975); Gerald R. Patterson and M. Elizabeth Gullion, *Living With Children: New Methods for Parents and Teachers*, revised edition (Champaign, Ill.: Research Press, 1971).

lips. "He must have deeper problems, and we thought you might help us to understand him better."

"Can you tell us what he does that makes you call him 'rebellious'?" Bill asked, probing for more concrete details.

"He's strong-willed. The minute we read Dobson's book about the strong-willed child we said, 'That's Clayton!' He doesn't seem to care what we want, and it's not getting any better."

Like most parents presenting their difficulties with children, the Bredemeiers used generalizations, which, in reality, gave us less information than we needed. By gently pressing them for specifics, we learned more, and by asking them to keep a three-day written record of every episode of Clayton's "bad" behavior, we learned much more. We decided together that whether Clayton, at age five, had "deep-seated psychological problems" remained to be seen. But it would be a good idea to begin by improving the relationship between this adopted child and his adoptive parents to the point where the anger we saw in Sam and Marian would be replaced by understanding love. To accomplish this, we all agreed that we would begin by training Clayton in obedience or compliance. With Clayton learning cheerful obedience, we all believed the angry resentment of the parents would cool down. In return, Clayton would feel better about himself and his parents.

Training Clayton in Compliance

The Bredemeiers were very nearly in despair, so they agreed to follow the program "to the letter," as Marian put it, and to meet with us regularly. They were to call us at any time and were even given a number where we could be reached if they needed on-the-spot advice.

Whether you are a total novice or an experienced veteran, please follow directions "to the letter," just as the Bredemeiers did. If you need professional help, a licensed psychologist can be called on for assistance. The steps we list are important—all of them. If you omit any of them you *may* get results anyhow, but then again you may *not*. Don't blame the program, look for the problem.

Here is what we all agreed to try to do: We would work together to install in their home a systematic reinforcement program using tokens that would, at least in the first stage of the program, lead to much improved obedience on Clayton's part. The Bredemeiers felt certain that they would respond very positively to the child if only he would cooperate with them even half the time.

Like the Bredemeiers, if you follow along step-by-step, you can create and install in your home a system of reinforcement with points or tokens that you can conveniently and happily use to carry out your parental ABC's. On page 137 and at the end of the book there are charts you can copy for every step of the program. We will take you through it step-by-step. Be sure to read the entire plan before you begin working it.

Follow These Simple Steps

Step 1: Get agreement. We were very happy that *both* Bredemeiers came together to see us about Clayton. Very often, one parent comes alone. Sometimes, people having difficulty believe the problem is in the child and that the function of the attending parent is to tell us about it and leave it up to us to work wonders in the child's behavior. But that isn't how it works. Wonders can be worked, all right, but not by a therapist. The project should be shouldered by the adults in the child's home. Before you begin any child-training program, discuss it—with each other and with other adults who might be living in your home and who will be expected to take any part in the program. Many a fine program has been sabotaged by an unknowing or uncooperative adult.

If you are a single parent, living alone, you should think all this through before you begin, determining what behaviors you need to change and what kind of change you need to bring about. If your children regularly visit a separated or divorced parent or another adult, try to obtain that person's cooperation with the program. If possible, involve him or her in the planning. We realize this can require tact, but we believe the results would be so valuable for the children it's worth the effort. Imagine your children being able to experience consistent rules and contingencies in both homes.

If you are one of two parents living together, it is vital to obtain your spouse's agreement to participate actively and enthusiastically. *A noncooperating spouse or other person living in the home can effectively undermine the program.* Work diligently on this step. Try your best to get everybody involved who might conceivably have some part in the training of your children.

What if, in spite of your best efforts, you can't obtain cooperation from pivotal persons? Well, then, apply one of the fundamental rules of successful living: *Do it yourself!* Do the best you can without help. You may experience difficulties, but don't give up and throw in the sponge. There's a job to do and you are going to try to cope with the problems as best you can. If another person in the home—or a noncustodial parent—has control of the reinforcers you are trying to utilize and that person is dispensing these reinforcers noncontingently (for example, satiating the children on pop and M&M's or giving them tons of money just to keep their approval), try to come up with reinforcers only you can offer. You can't think of any? How about precious time with you alone—your companionship, special dishes you can prepare better than anyone else, the bike to which only you possess the key, activities you can introduce the child to better than anybody else around, like playing ball or cooking or knitting or skiing or fishing? When it comes to planning, think, think, think.

Step 2: Get specific. We insisted that Clayton's parents quit using vague abstractions and required them to describe his offending behavior in such concrete terms that we could visualize the little boy blithely ignoring their expressed wishes, doing exactly what he wanted to, and even seeming to deliberately locate the lines they drew so he could step over them. When they agreed to log specific behaviors for a few days, their written descriptions enabled us to determine precisely what was going on and we could determine together what had to be changed. You too need to abandon broad generalizations like, "She doesn't respect us." Determine exactly what behaviors you want to work on, defining them explicitly—like, "Colleen told her father to 'Chill out' when he asked her to explain why she was late getting home."

Specifically described actions (words, too) to be changed are what we call *target behaviors*. The process of nailing down precisely what you want to change is often called *pinpointing*. Don't go off half-cocked here without making sure you have pinpointed the behaviors of interest well enough so they can be readily identified by the child and by every involved adult. If you thoughtlessly decide to work on something like, "He has to stop being so insolent," you may have troubles later over whether or not a particular sentence emitted by the child was "insolent" or not. It is much better to pinpoint by specifying exactly what you mean like this: "He is not to say 'I won't!' when asked to do something by an adult in the home."

Pinpointing Replaces Generalizations

Here are some more examples for you:

Instead of	Specify
Becomes more obedient.	Does what he is asked to do without arguing, complaining, or procrastinating.
Helps more around the house.	Dusts dining room furniture twice a week to Mom's satisfaction on inspection.
Gets to bed on time	Begins at 8:15 P.M. without prompting to get ready for bed, brush teeth, take bath, put on pajamas, and be in bed with light out by 9:00 P.M.
Becomes more polite.	Says "please" whenever she makes requests of anyone in the home, says "thank you" whenever anyone in the home responds to her requests.

Does not belch at the table without covering and closing her mouth.

Sits down at the table, puts napkin in lap, waits to eat until after prayer, folds hands, bows head, participates in table prayer.

You might want to do some observation and recording of your child's actual behavior as Clayton's parents did in order to determine what precisely you'd like to change. As with anything else we're accustomed to in our everyday surroundings, we can become so oblivious to a child's bad behavior that we don't even see it when it happens—or else we're so vaguely aware of it, we can't readily pinpoint it. Take a few days to observe and record everything your child does or doesn't do that you find undesirable. Writing down the precise form of the child's actual behavior is good practice and will help you to specify precisely how you want that behavior to change.

"Shall we tell Clayton we're keeping records of his bad conduct?" asked Marian. "What if he notices we're writing it down?"

"Probably not, Marian," Candy answered. "We recommend that at this stage, you keep what you are doing to yourselves. If the child knows you are making an issue of his behavior, he may change temporarily, with the result that your records won't be accurate."

Step 3: Count. At our next session, Marian presented us with an excellent record of Clayton's offending behaviors. She and Sam had pinpointed the behavior by observing it and describing it accurately. The next step would be to count. We decided to work first on obedience of compliance with Clayton. So the Bredemeiers agreed to count on paper every single instance of noncompliance or disobedience for three days. We asked them to be sure to give Clayton some commands he could choose to disobey. One of the problems posed by parents whose children are not very obedient is that they have backed off and frequently formed the habit of not giving any real requests to the child, since it is so nonreinforcing for them to do so. We have to prime the pump, so to speak. After you have pinpointed the behavior or behaviors you want to change and the sort of change you are interested in obtaining, it's time to get an accurate record of how often the bad behavior occurs or how often the child fails to do what is expected. This is referred to as a *base rate*, because it gives you a starting point from which to measure changes. If you don't really know how many of your commands your child now obeys, how will you be certain there's improvement later? So keep a tally card handy and every time the bad behavior occurs, make a mark on your card (preferably when the child isn't observing). Or if you are targeting something like obedience, you should actually create the occasions for it by being sure to give plenty of commands.

For instance, if you choose to work on compliance:

- Be sure to give the child at least ten requests per day, beginning when you start counting to get a base rate.
- Keep close track of his responses to your commands or requests, including every episode of compliance as well as those times when he performs the request but only with a disagreeable attitude or perhaps after much procrastinating on his part or lots of nagging or threats on yours, or of course, when he doesn't do what is requested at all.
- Three representative days may be enough to get a base rate. This depends on how frequent the opportunities are for the behavior to occur. If it has to do with behavior in church, for instance, you may need to take three weeks to collect three representative days. Or if you're visiting Aunt Nellie, your frequency counts may be nonrepresentative, so you may do better to wait until you're home and have a rather normal time period in which to collect data.

Save your results. They will enable you to know for certain whether, and to what extent, what you are doing is working.

Step 4: Choose good reinforcers. Now comes a time for some really creative thinking. What will you use for *backup reinforcers*? The Bredemeiers had no problem here. Clayton loved raisins. He would consider it a special treat if Marian gave him a little cup with raisins in it to carry around and munch on, one at a time. So they selected raisins for backup reinforcement. Clayton would get three raisins for each point he earned by compliance. They decided to give him another option. He would be allowed to exchange his rubber rings for Dr. Seuss stories read by Sam if he preferred. A story would be worth five points. They did not think Clayton would make sense out of marks on a chart at first, so we decided to use tokens. Marian had plenty of rubber rings from old canning jars, so we determined that jar rings would be tokens and that Clayton would be given a jar ring each time he complied with a request. Later we learned that the five-year-old was delighted with the jar rings themselves, that he carried them around like bracelets on his arms, and only after a day or two was he willing to exchange them for raisins and stories.

As you consider and choose backup reinforcers, a conference is in order with both parents and/or other involved adults. "We will be giving Johnny tokens (points, gold stars, plastic disks) whenever he does the target behaviors properly. What will work best as backup reinforcers?" As you consider this question, use all your knowledge of your child and his habits. What does he do when he is free to do whatever he wishes? You've got a reinforcer! To use it, however, you'll have to be able to prevent his doing it without having earned enough points. Marian had to stop giving Clayton raisins whenever he asked for them and to begin requiring him to earn jar rings in exchange for raisins.

Think about your child's habits. What does he like? What does he request? What would he like to have much more of than he is now given? Think of privileges, things, and money. Come up with several good age-appropriate reinforcers.

Reinforcers

Here are some actual examples of reinforcers others have chosen. You may find some of them very useful:

- choose the dessert for dinner
- take the family to a fast-food restaurant
- trip to Dairy Queen
- stay up half an hour past bedtime
- go to zoo
- half an hour on family computer
- use of family car (if licensed)
- take driver training program
- new football, shoulder pads, etc. . . . .
- new doll
- new computer program
- half an hour of TV time (for parent-approved shows only)
- have a friend stay overnight
- 15 minutes of telephone time
- own phone line, in-room phone
- puppy or kitten
- game with Dad or Mom
- Mom reads a story
- friend over for dinner
- new book
- money (five or ten cents per point)
- new clothes

Use your knowledge of your child, your imagination, and your own rules and norms to select appropriate backup reinforcers. If you don't believe children should ever have sugar, you probably won't want to use candy. On the other hand, a child who hasn't been given much sweet stuff will probably find M&M's *very* reinforcing! And remember, whatever reinforcers you select, be sure to present them with enthusiasm, praise, recognition, appreciation and lots of love, because our aim is to rely *almost exclusively* on such *social reinforcers* in the end.

Choose several reinforcers you would like to offer your child so she will have a selection to pick from when she has tokens or points to exchange. That's one advantage of using points or tokens—you aren't limited to just one backup reinforcer. So if the child is temporarily uninterested in one of the rewards on her menu, there are still other attractive choices available to her. Some things are reinforcing to most children. Money, for instance, rewards nearly all humans old enough to realize that it can be exchanged for numerous goods. Parental time and attention, though parents often do not realize it, has universal reinforcing value. Playing a game with Dad or Mom, hearing favorite stories from them, baking cookies with Mom, baking bread with Dad, going fishing with Dad, taking a hike in the woods with Mom—are privileges most children will work hard to obtain, particularly if the parents participate joyously.

Step 5: Determine how many points you will award. Next you must determine how many points or tokens you will award the child for various good behaviors. This can be any convenient number, completely arbitrarily determined. Usually, if the behavior is likely to occur very frequently, one token or one point per occasion is convenient. If the behavior is rare, or if it seems as if it will be particularly difficult to elicit for any reason, two, three, or more points may be awarded for it. The numbers in this game are completely up to you. The Bredemeiers simply gave Clayton one jar ring for every episode of compliant behavior. Later, when they resolved to move on to teaching him to put himself to bed, they gave him two jar rings whenever he completed the entire procedure on time.

Step 6: Determine the value of each point. What really matters more than the number of points you offer per behavior is the *value* you establish for each point or token. Here, remember to err on the side of generosity at first. Sam and Marian began with a very simple program. They had already determined that each jar ring would be worth three raisins. When we came to Step 6, they concluded that one Dr. Seuss story read by Sam would cost Clayton five jar rings (an easy half day's compliance, given if his parents continued to create at least ten requests every day). Another of our clients, Roberta Walker, had a problem with this part of the design. She worried about the possibility of giving her son, Mark, too much. "But," she would say, "just feeding the dog isn't worth that much! Why should I give him 25 cents for *that*?" Or, "He gets points for just saying 'please' and 'thank you'! That means he can make lots of money just by asking for things and adding 'please' to his requests. What a racket!"

Many parents think the way Roberta did. According to old habits, they've always tried to spend as little as possible for whatever they bought. In a market context, that's very wise. It's called *prudence*. But in this program you must want to give as much as possible! You must catch on, as Roberta did later, to the fact that *you want the child to be greatly reinforced*. Don't forget that you hope strongly for the child to successfully earn lots of positive reinforcement. Why? Because, according to the law of reinforcement, every time the child does the desired behavior and receives reinforcement for it, the behavior grows stronger. So don't worry too much about the possibility of giving the child too much reinforcement. Plan your backups to be generous. And give them happily.

For the most part, exchange tokens or points for backups whenever the child has the proper number and wants to exchange them. Of course, reinforcers like time with Dad or Mom can't be had "on demand," because they depend on time available and the child must understand that. But when it comes to paying up, don't procrastinate, or string the child along. Pay promptly. If you don't, your credit won't be in good standing with your child. The result of "welshing" on your debts will be a failed program.

What we've just said doesn't mean you can't offer some backup rewards that will cost the child a lot of points and a good deal of effort. You can, and if the child wants it bad enough, he may save his points for it. A special vacation trip, a new bike, a set of bunk beds, an automobile, driving lessons, can all be used as backups costing large numbers of points. If the child wants to save points for them, that's his option. But most children need first to experience how the program works with more readily usable rewards. So other, less expensive rewards should probably be used for your first backups. Later, along with them, a large, expensive, long-term reward can be added.

Step 7: Presenting the plan to your child. When you have decided on the shape of the program, it's time to present it to your child. Just how you will go about this depends on the circumstances and the child's age and maturity level. At the outset, Sam Bredemeier simply explained to Clayton that Dad and Mom were going to work together to help him learn to do what they asked him. They explained that every time Clayton did exactly as one of them requested without making excuses or fussing or delaying, they would give him a ring. They showed him how the rings would fit on his arm and they actually gave him a couple and allowed him to exchange them then and there for some raisins. Then they suggested that they try out the scenario and asked Clayton to simply open the hall door. When he did it right away they praised him abundantly and gave him a ring. He promptly slipped it on his arm and asked for another command. This game went on for a couple of additional trials. Clayton couldn't wait for his next request.

When you explain the program to your child, do not present it as optional. Not: "Would you be willing to do so-and-so to get candy?" Instead, tell the child what is going to happen: "Lately, I haven't enjoyed asking you to do things for me because you have said 'No!' or maybe just forgotten to do some of the things I've asked you to do. I've been keeping track. Yesterday, for instance, I asked you to do ten different things for me. You did what I asked only six times, and once in a while you complained or argued with me before you finally did what I asked. I didn't like the complaining. And I didn't like the four times you didn't obey me at all. So I'd like to try something new. I'd like you to do what I ask you to do right away, without arguing or complaining or putting it off. And whenever you do that, I am going to put a point on this chart for you. You will be able to use the points when you wish. You can exchange them for TV time, for money, or for having friends over. Here's how it will work. Ready? Let's try it a couple of times.

Will you please go and get me a pencil? Thank you very much. That's exactly what I mean! I really enjoyed asking you to do that and having you get me a pencil without arguing or complaining. You did it right away too. That makes me feel better already. Now I'll use the pencil to give you a point. If you wish you can exchange that point for ten cents right now or you can save it for other things. I'm going to put your point chart on the refrigerator so you can always see how many points you've earned by just doing what I ask you to do, how many points you have spent for things you like, and how many points you still have left. Do you want to ask me any questions?"

For especially noncompliant kids, or kids with very short attention spans, it might be best to have a roll of nickels or dimes and begin without reference to a chart or to points. Just dispense coins for a few days. Then switch to the chart, explaining that the points will always be just as good as coins, because the child can exchange them for money if he wishes. But because he might want something else sometimes, you're giving him several options. Show him the list of backup reinforcers you've come up with on the chart and explain how many points each one will cost.

Step 8: Remember to add social reinforcement. "Sam, what did you do when you gave Clayton his rings? I see by the chart he's earned ten rings every day except Monday and yesterday when he only earned seven and eight respectively," said Bill when Clayton and Marian proudly presented the record of Clayton's compliance rate. Sam had computed it: 79 percent! He was obeying roughly eight out of ten requests without arguing, complaining, or procrastinating! Just for the record—and so you can appreciate why his parents were almost incredulous and enormously pleased after they had used the program for just a week—Clayton had begun the program with a very low compliance base rate of 47 percent. He wasn't obeying even half the time! With such a marvelous result, the Bredemeiers were elated.

"So what did you do when you gave your child his rings and his raisins and stories?" Bill pressed the point.

"Well, I put the ring in his hands. And I read to him when he had the points. He consumed most of his points in raisins."

"Sam," Candy interjected, "I want you to couple your tangible reinforcers with abundant expressions of your pleasure in Clayton and his performance. We call these expressions *'social reinforcers.'* Remembering to give them freely, enthusiastically, is the real mainstay of this program. Eventually, you'll be withdrawing the rings and the charts, the tangible rewards, and getting Clayton to behave properly for nothing except your expressions of pleasure. To do that, we begin right now to give him such social rewards *along with* other reinforcers *every time* Clayton complies according to the rules." The Bredemeiers, pleased as they were, had been so taken with the mechanics of the program they had been rather emotionally constricted in their interactions with their little boy. Now we were urging them to relax and express joy and pleasure in him whenever they caught him doing good, and especially when they gave him tangible reinforcement.

You too may easily forget or, worse yet, routinize the giving of social reinforcers. Omitting them or turning them into a perfunctory social ritual can happen because, especially at first, the tangible reinforcement offered in your program will have such power. You may see such gratifying results from points, or jar rings, and backup reinforcers that you'll forget altogether the importance of your own expressions of delight and pleasure in the face of your child's successful efforts. Remember, you want to introduce enthusiastic praise along with other rewards right away at the very beginning, and give some thought to maintaining a high and meaningful level of social rewards throughout your child's years of training.

More Social Reinforcers

Here are some additional examples of social reinforcers. Use your own words; if you wish, create your own expressions of delight. Turn back to Chapter 11 to review some of our suggestions. Here are some more examples of what we mean:

- *Give your child a simple "Thank you."* "I want you to know how much you've helped me by sorting the clothes and putting them in the washer. I really appreciate your being so willing and helping me so much! Thanks!"
- *Don't forget to smile.* Accompany all rewards and all praise and approval with a positive, smiling, happy attitude and expression.
- *Hugs, kisses, touches, pats on the back.* Most children love to be touched by their parents because they love their parents. Express your pleasure and good feelings toward the child with a hug, a squeeze, a pat on the back, a hand on the shoulder, a kiss. Fathers especially are remembered by many adults as lacking in physical expressions of love and affection. Dad, even if you didn't get much of this from your own father, give it generously to your children. It will make a huge difference in your relationships with them and it will serve as a potent positive reward.
- *Give plenty of praise. Don't be stingy with it.* "You set the table so well tonight I thought I was dining at the best restaurant in town! Beautiful job!"
- *Express your pleasure in the child and the conduct.* "I'll bet you can't even guess how good it makes me feel when you do things like that for me. I feel happy because of you!"

  "I love you so much I'm thrilled when you do things like that!"

  "Because I love you more than anything, I feel really glad when you do what I ask like that."
- *Brag about the child to other people.* In his presence, tell about the child's accomplishments. "Do you know what happened to me today? I took Jacob to the bookstore and he read a whole book to me when we sat together in the kids' section. You wouldn't believe how that boy can read!"
- *Give him applause.* After all, you applaud all sorts of per-

formers you probably don't even know. Why not some applause for that child who's trying so hard to win your approval? "Wow! Very impressive! The lawn looks like velvet, you mowed it so incredibly well! Terrific!"

- *Put down your book, your newspaper, even your work and give your child your precious attention and approval.* "Rob, I hear you can add fractions. Could you show me a sample? . . . Man, that's terrific! And you're only in the fifth grade. How'd you ever get so good so fast? I like the way you did that!"

Step 9: What to do when it stops working. You knew it was inevitable. The day nearly always arrives when the child decides, as we would sometimes, that it just isn't worth it today. She has lots of points. She really doesn't feel like washing the dishes tonight or brushing her teeth or whatever. So she tells you she isn't going to do it and she doesn't care about earning the points. She has all the points she needs and for now she'd rather read.

There are several solutions. But first, consider how sensible the child's decision is from her point of view. She's earned enough rewards offered by the program, so it's more rewarding at this point to read a book than to earn a quarter or an additional TV time that can just as well be earned tomorrow or the next day. You can expect that one day your child will make this discovery.

Here are some remedies you'll probably think of yourself:

- You could add reinforcers you know she wants so badly she'd rather earn them than read.
- You could make her exchange points for reading time, making reading a backup reinforcer.
- You could introduce fines or response costs into your program.

Let's look at using *response costs*. We recommend it often. What it amounts to is that when a child chooses not to do the good behavior they've been learning to do, or they resume old unwanted conduct, they have points subtracted from their balance. In other words, they get fined.

If you don't do this, most children will eventually come to the point where, after a little calculation, they decide they have temporarily achieved enough points and/or backup reinforcers and that for them at that moment it would be more reinforcing to resume their old ways. There may be times when this would be no disaster from your point of view, and you can just wait until they want to resume working for the backups you've offered. But there may be times when you don't want to tolerate *any* resumption of old ways: for example, disobedience, disrespect, omitting positive health and hygiene habits. Safety and health might be better served by a proven punishment: *fine them*.

Here's what you do. If you're using tokens or points, simply declare that from this point on, noncompliance won't be tolerated at all, even though the child had made wonderful progress with compliance. So you'll continue to award one token for every episode of compliance, but you will take away *two* tokens or *two* points for every episode of noncompliance. You guarantee that the child cannot comfortably continue performing the unwanted behavior (or omitting the wanted behavior) by making the price of doing wrong higher than the reward for doing right. Your point chart should have a section where you can list conduct you are planning to charge points for and the amount of the cost for each unwanted response. All other things being equal, the results you get will convince you that occasional fines help a lot because punishment—which is what fines are—does change behavior.

Some Cautions

- Do not begin any program with a child by including response costs or fines right away. You want the first couple of weeks or so to bring the child nothing but enormously positive experiences and big batches of reinforcement. Wait until your child has shown that she earns points *and exchanges them for backup reinforcers* before you introduce fines.

- Do not continue a program in which the child is running out of points or, worse, going toward a negative balance. No negative balances are ever allowed. That means you do not allow the child to have a backup reinforcer for which he hasn't enough points "on credit." Nor do you allow the child's point balance to enter the red due to fines. If this is happening, there is a problem. Look for it. Are your backup reinforcers enticing enough? Does the child have plenty of them without doing the program, or has he stopped being interested in the ones you're offering? Look over the situation. Find the problem. Make some changes.

- Do not administer fines with put-downs, negative comments, bitterness, anger, or rage. Calm down if the child's behavior has upset you! Then, calmly point out the wrong conduct. Say, "You complained when I asked you to pick up your shoes. That's noncompliance. It will cost you two points," and then record the cost on the chart or ask the child to give you the requisite number of tokens. Stay calm. Do not smile, and do not make a federal case out of the transgression because you might actually be reinforcing undesirable actions with attention if you do.

Step 10: Aim at getting off the program! This is not a "step" so much as a trend you want to be aware of throughout the program, a direction you are aiming at. Eventually you want to dispense with the token economy. Not that you can't feel free to utilize it in whole or in part in the future if the need arises, but you and your children want to discover that love and positive social rewards can produce the results desired in improved behavior. So the aim of the program is to get off the program and to replace it with nothing but social reinforcement backed up occasionally by other rewards given spontaneously.

Do not let the program stagnate. Many parents have found that the point system works for them and that it is easy. In fact, they get better results more easily than they have ever dreamed possible, and they get them so fast and using such proven methods, they are inclined to settle back and let the system work itself. And in detaching emotionally and intellectually from the process of training their offspring, they let the program deteriorate until it's pretty useless. Then they quietly let it die by not recording points, by not creating new and fresh backup reinforcers (although their children and their desires and needs change daily as they grow and mature), by failing to deliver on promised reinforcement, and by resuming old habits of nagging and threatening or even just looking the other way when their children are not exhibiting mature and God-pleasing conduct.

Keep Creating New Ideas

Along with addressing problems as they arise, creating new ideas for reinforcement, new ways to earn points, and, occasionally adding additional fines or response costs, keep working toward the end of the program. Don't forget the praise, thanks, and love. As you do this, gradually phase out the giving of points and tangible rewards for behaviors that have been well learned and which the child will continue with only your recognition, approval, and pleasure as rewards. When you see that your child's compliance has become a habit, say something like, "You have become so wonderfully obedient, we aren't going to need to work on that anymore. I really am thrilled with you and with how you nearly always do as I ask without any fuss and right away! Let's take that one off the chart and instead, I'd like to show my appreciation by taking you to a bookstore where you can get any book you'd like." Have the child himself erase or line out the item on his point chart. For some behaviors you may want to reduce the point value and give a half point less instead of a full point for them. Make the effort to increase social rewards as you phase out points. And occasionally tell the child you want to take him out for lunch or buy him a toy or take him to a ball game "because I appreciate what you've been doing to keep your room neat as a pin lately!"

WEEK OF __4-5__ BEHAVIOR CHART FOR __andy__

New Behavior Description	Point Value	ONE HASH MARK FOR EACH EPISODE							Point Total
		SUN	MON	TUE	WED	THU	FRI	SAT	
Complete homework	3	|	|	|	|	|			15
Brush teeth	1	||	|	|\		||			7
Walk dog	1			|	|	|		|	4
Makes bed well	2	|	|	|		|		|	10
POINTS EARNED THIS WEEK									36
POINT BALANCE CARRIED FORWARD FROM LAST WEEK									6
TOTAL POINTS EARNED									42

Undesirable Behavior Description	Point Value	ONE HASH MARK FOR EACH EPISODE							Point Total
		SUN	MON	TUE	WED	THU	FRI	SAT	
Talks back	3							⊤⊣⊣	15
Hits sister	5							|	5
TOTAL POINTS LOST THIS WEEK									20

TOTAL POINTS AVAILABLE (points earned minus points lost)	22

Privileges For Points	Point Value	ONE HASH MARK FOR EACH EPISODE							Point Total
		SUN	MON	TUE	WED	THU	FRI	SAT	
Money – 25¢	5								
Computer – ½ hr.	2	||						||	8
Friend overnight	10							|	10
TOTAL POINTS USED FOR PRIVILEGES THIS WEEK									18
POINT BALANCE (points available minus points used)									4

Eventually, if you will keep eliminating and reducing points awarded, you can move beyond the point system. This does not mean you can move beyond rewards. All human relationships include exchange of rewards.

But it does mean that your child *is* maturing in responsibility—and that should keep you smiling for a long time!

Using a Point Chart

You will need to construct some kind of chart if you use points. We offer you a model that you may copy freely or modify to create your own. (There is a blank chart at the end of this book.) The essential ingredients (besides the dates and days, the name of the child, and the title of the chart) are descriptions of the new behaviors to be acquired by the child, the number of points to be awarded for each occurrence of one of them, and a way of counting how many times each new behavior occurs on each day of the week coverd by the chart. Places to total up points earned are also needed.

You must add a place to list reinforcers or privileges for which the child can exchange the points she has earned, a place to note the number of points each privilege will cost the child, places to total the cost of used points, and the balance of points left over at the end of the week. After the program is rolling and the child is doing new behaviors and earning points, you may begin to use the spaces for fines when unwanted behaviors occur.

On the previous page is an example of the chart. Although it includes a section for fines, we don't want you to begin the program using them. You may construct a chart just like it yourself if you wish.

Please remember not to begin the program with the chart for undesirable behavior. Wait with fines for a couple of weeks at least! The child needs to have a very positive experience earning reinforcers *first*. Later, when he has a good balance of points, you can begin introducing fines for unwanted behaviors.

III

Dealing With Common Problems

14

Bedtime

Now that you've read about an effective way to shape your child's behavior, *it's time to apply principles and procedures*.

Fortunately, the behavior most parents run up against are common. Very few children, creative though their minds may be, have invented brand-new quandaries for us, their parents. Whatever your own particular challenge may be, it might be comforting to know that others have been there before you. Teasing little sister must have originated with Seth, while refusal to go to bed and stay there is a parent-buster reinvented with every new generation since the flood.

There Are *Solutions*

There are solutions. Most parents are familiar with vexing questions like: How do you deal with your four-year-old when he makes up a lie to get himself out of trouble? Whining, temper-tantrums, "forgetting" chores, neglecting personal hygiene, sloppy table manners, biting, hitting and scratching others, lying, stealing, and negativism may seem like unsolvable conundrums. They're not. You are well equipped with what it takes to handle all this and more. Let's move ahead by discussing the major difficulties one at a time.

Bedtime

With a sigh of relief, Nadine sank onto the sofa beside Bob.

"Did you get her into bed at last?" asked Bob.

"I hope so. She kept finding another toy to rearrange, another doll to tuck in, another book from which she'd prefer to have her bedtime story read. After she finally climbed into bed, she went through the old routine—well, you know how it goes!" Nadine sighed.

"You were going to have her in bed with the light out by 8:30," Bob muttered. In fact, this tiny four-year-old had managed to squeeze another half hour or so out of her parents.

"Mommy, I want a drink of water!"

Both parents cringed. They'd hoped they'd hear no more of Renee's little voice that night.

Bob decided it was time for *authority* to take over: "No water! Go to sleep, Renee! I don't want to have to come up there, and you'll be sorry if I do!"

It seemed to work. Renee didn't answer. As the frazzled couple settled into their reading, they hoped they'd achieved their goal. But, looking up from the newspaper, Bob saw a tiny tearful face standing in the doorway in her little nightie. Guilt swept over him. He'd hurt his daughter's feelings! "All right. Get back in bed. I'll get you a drink. But if you yell or get up one more time, I'm going to spank you. Do you understand?"

Renee did understand, of course. But she had also learned from her parents that they threatened several times before approaching the danger zone. So she waited a few minutes after drinking her water, then called to inform her parents that she couldn't sleep. Also available in her repertoire should she decide to pull them out: "I'm afraid there's a monster in here." "I have to go to the bathroom." "I forgot to brush my teeth." "I'm hungry." "I want to get in your big bed for a while." All in all, Renee managed to prolong her bedtime interactions with her parents until 9:48 P.M.—a record hour and twenty-eight minutes from the time Nadine had begun the dreaded process of getting her daughter to retire for the night.

Most parents encounter similar if not identical difficulties with one or more of their offspring. Many children do not like to go to bed for the simple reason that bedtime constitutes a removal from reinforcement. Consider that parental attention, being with the family, playing with toys, looking at books and watching TV are reinforcing to a child. So when you announce that it's bedtime, you herald the removal of powerful reinforcers. Most children would rather wear themselves out until they virtually fall asleep playing than interrupt their activities to go to bed.

You need to understand this basic point so you don't buy into the child's efforts to convince you that powerful needs make it necessary to defer going to sleep. You must not be manipulated by such revelations as, "I'm thirsty," or "I need to brush my teeth." More truthful would be, "I want to prolong reinforcement as long as possible."

You *can* train your child to go to bed on time and go to sleep thereafter without repeatedly interrupting your precious respite and rest at day's end. Though it may not seem possible, you can do it. Here's how:

Five Procedures for Bedtime Peace

First, you must choose a time when you and the child can sit down and talk. Don't choose bedtime. Then explain that you haven't been happy with the situation: "I don't like it when you find ways to avoid going to bed on time. I want you to go to bed when I tell you and be in bed under the covers with the light off by 8:30 (or whatever). After that, I don't want you to get up or to call me. If you have to go to the bathroom, you may get up and do it, but don't call me. Just get back into bed and go to sleep."

Second, ask the child if he wants a drink of water at bedtime and if he does, tell him to remember to get it before he goes to bed. Make a glass available for his use in the bathroom. Ask the child if he has any questions about how this will work. Answer them, teach him to make provision for his bedtime wants and needs before 8:30. ("If you want to put your toys to bed before you go, you can start that at 7:30. Do you want me to let you know when it's 7:30?") Children who are able to tell time ought to be taught to watch the time for themselves and get started with their routine without being prompted.

If you are using a point or token system, tell the child on what basis you will give her points. For example, "I'm going to give you one point for starting to go to bed without being told. I'll give you a reminder for one or two nights; then you will have to start getting to bed yourself without a reminder in order to get a point."

Third, announce that "we will practice right now" and walk through the entire routine with your child, letting him know that it's just pretend and that he won't have to actually go to sleep now because it's daytime, but that it's important to practice so he gets it right tonight. Praise him happily for successes along the way.

Read these suggested responses, and see if they may work for you: "That's right. You remembered to put your toys away in plenty of time. [If you are using points . . .] I'm going to give you a point for remembering to put your toys away."

"Good for you. You remembered to brush your teeth before you got into bed—and you even remembered to give yourself a drink of water! I'm giving you two points for doing those two things yourself."

"Wow! You even remembered to say your prayers. That's great. I'm so proud of you I'm going to give you a point for remembering it yourself!"

"You've done this so well, I'm going to start the hardest part now. I'm going to leave you in bed and go to the living room and sit down. You must stay in bed until you fall sound asleep and have beautiful dreams."

In the morning, let your child know how many points or tokens he's earned.

Fourth, remember to reward your child for successes along the way at night. Expressions of praise and your positive feelings about his efforts are rewarding if you make them very enthusiastic and upbeat! If you are using points or tokens for reinforcers, give them generously. When he stays in bed and falls asleep, you'll have to give him his points, tokens, or other rewards in the morning, first thing. Remember the praise then, too!

Fifth, you must be sure to punish your child for not getting to bed on time or for getting out of bed except to go to the bathroom after lights out. If you are using points or tokens, institute response costs or fines and actually take away tokens or points while the child can see you do it. If you are not using points or tokens, announce that a routinely granted privilege will be taken away tomorrow: "You got out of bed and came to the living room. It makes me feel very bad when you do that after you're in bed. I'm going to take away two of your points for that." (If you are not using points or tokens, remove a privilege.) "Tomorrow you won't be able to watch *Sesame Street*. I hope that will help you remember not to get out of bed." Then make the child return to bed immediately. Do not give attention or respond to requests! Do not give water or fulfill any other requests! Insist that the child go to bed and stay there and do not give in.

"I Want to Sleep in Your Bed"

Some parents have discovered that their preschooler prefers their bed to her own. "I want to sleep with you and Mommy," or "I'm scared. Can I get in bed with you?" In the middle of the night, when you've been awakened from a sound sleep and it's dark and cold, it's terribly hard to make yourself deal with the child's fears and disobedience. So you say, "All right. Get in. But be quiet and go to sleep." You put the little one between you and your mate, and go back to dreamland. Many parents have regretted this!

If you allow the child to get into your bed, you will be reinforcing her for behavior you may find hard to eliminate later. Instead, get out of bed, pick up your small child, and take her gently but firmly back to her own bed. Allay any fears, cover her up and tell her, "This is your bed, darling. This is where you sleep. Not in our bed. We love you. Now go back to sleep. I'll tuck you in nice and cozy and warm."

Firm but gentle refusal will eliminate this behavior.

And diligent work *will* bring bedtime under control— *yours*!

15

No More Tantrums

Every once in a while you may run into an adult who has never outgrown the habit of throwing tantrums. Full-grown chaps and physically developed matrons who, when thwarted, howl, hurl cups, clam up and pout for hours or days, are emotional toddlers. They relate like two-year-olds because no one ever taught them to grow up and use more effective social behaviors!

We ourselves have met too many of these overgrown children. We call them to your attention because we want to motivate you for the task of eliminating temper tantrums *now* from your child's repertoire.

What's a Tantrum?

Although there is no precise, scientific definition, we all know a tantrum when we see it. The child's activity level escalates suddenly. He is no longer soft spoken, no longer even whining—now he is shrieking in a fit of outrage. His physical activity level also accelerates. He bangs his head, holds his breath, or pounds his fists. He turns red in the face as he screams and shrieks. The whole event may even persuade you that he is out of control, that he is experiencing an attack of some kind which he is powerless to bring

147

to a halt—unless of course you give him what he wants or stop insisting on what you want. If you let this performance frighten you, you're apt to give in to the child, thus reinforcing him *and* strengthening the tantrum habit.

Training for Tantrums

Such is the life of a parent that we sometimes unintentionally train our children to have tantrums. Imagine your two-year-old asking you for a cookie. It's 5:00, and supper will be served at 5:30. You want her to eat a good dinner so you say, "Not now, sweetheart. We'll be eating supper soon."

Instead of accepting your answer, she whines, "I want a cookie, please, please, *please*, Mommy."

Again you refuse. She begins crying. You don't respond. She cries louder. You tell yourself you can't tolerate her wails, not tonight, so you break down and give in: "Oh, all *right*! Now go play and leave me alone. Here's one cookie. And that's positively all you get."

Happily, the tot munches her cookie and goes back to her toys. But you, though enjoying the release, are haunted by guilt. You shouldn't have given her that cookie! So you resolve not to give in the next time.

But the next time, she intensifies her demands. As you hang tough, she gets louder. On this occasion, you may hold out until dinnertime. But on the day after, she screams, cries, and bangs her head. This is more than you bargained for, so you part with a cookie.

Each time, you are rewarding her for becoming *more intense*! Do you see how you can gradually reward her for increasingly intense behavior? Can you see how you strengthen demanding, pounding, stomping, and screaming? We'll look at how you can reverse this process. But first, let's examine some different kinds of tantrums.

Types of Tantrums

Most children who have acquired the habit of responding to reality with tantrum behavior are trying to get something from another person. They have discovered that tantrums work. Adults, and sometimes other children, give in to their demands. So, by having tantrums, they get what they want when all else fails. Perhaps not every time, but even if tantrums work only occasionally, such sporadic success causes the tantrum habit to grow stronger. One reason children have tantrums is to *get something they want.*

Another occasion for the tantrums of some children (and immature adults) is the refusal of the environment to work the way they want it to. When the jigsaw puzzle won't come together, the "tantrumite" pounds the table and screams in sheer frustration. Sometimes, the environment, in the person of an adult, responds by making things better. *So the child learns to throw a tantrum when frustrated and comes to believe a tantrum will remove the frustration!*

Tantrums also occur as a response to being forced to do what the child doesn't want to do. When you insist that he pick up his toys, he thwarts your will by "falling apart" with a tantrum. Then *he doesn't have to do what he doesn't want to do.*

You can deduce from what has been said that the wrong response to tantrums is to reward or reinforce the child for throwing his fit. If you are fortunate enough to be reading this book before your child has developed any tantrum behavior, you can very likely prevent its getting started by forcing yourself *not* to break down and *not* to give in to intensified demands by your toddler.

If you say, "No cookie," stick to your guns no matter what Junior does to persuade you. And stem the tide of guilt feelings! You're not doing him any harm by your refusal. Stay calm and ignore the child and his requests. *Ignore* means *pay no attention to.* Do not reinforce the child. Don't look at him or speak to him. You might even go to another room. If intense pestering continues, send the young child to time out.[1] If you have to, pick him up and put him in the time out place and make him stay there. Remember, offer him as little attention or conversation as possible.

---

[1]See Chapter 10 for instructions on using time out.

When a Tantrum Expresses Futility Feelings

When the child throws a tantrum because the box won't come open or the puzzle won't come together or the house he's building collapses, you can understand his frustrated feelings. But don't reinforce the behavior. Simply say, "When you calm down, I'll be glad to help you." And then pay no attention whatever as long as the tantrum continues. *After* the child calms down you may offer help. Later, you may want to explain that you are not going to help when he throws a tantrum because you don't like tantrums. You do like to be asked politely for help, and you really want to do all you can for him when he asks you nicely.

Tantrums to Get Out of Doing What He Doesn't Want to Do

If the tantrum occurs when the child doesn't want to obey you, ignore it. Do not reinforce it even with attention, and wait until it ends. You may use time out if necessary. But then, when the tantrum ends, be sure to insist calmly and firmly that he carry out your original request.

We realize you will want to avoid another tantrum so much you'll be sorely tempted to forget the whole thing, but that is a major mistake. What you will have taught him by your backing down is that tantrums work.

If he meets your request with another tantrum, ignore it again and wait until it's over. Do *not* give in. Make certain he doesn't evade the necessity of obedience by his tantrum behavior *no matter how often* he resorts to it.

Remember to reward him with powerful praise and recognition when he does calm down and do what you asked him to do. "I really like the way you did that without screaming or kicking. It makes me feel so good, I want to do something for you. How about a cookie [or a story, or a romp in the woods]?"

A Recipe for Tantrum Control

To sum up—if you have a child who has tantrums:

- Do not reward him for having them. Remember, stick to

your guns if you have refused him something. Make him carry out your request if he's thrown a tantrum rather than obey you. Don't talk to him or try to soothe him. Don't even look at him. Leave the room if you have to. As a last resort, send the child to time out or, if necessary, pick him up and put him in time out.

- Do tell yourself the truth: You are not guilty of child abuse by not responding to the tantrum. Your child can control himself and will learn to when his tantrums stop working for him.
- Do respond to the child when he stops his tantrum behavior. Praise him and reward him for *not* screaming or kicking.

16

Lying

It has been commonplace in sexual abuse cases to hear people say "Children don't lie" to validate child testimony. Unfortunately, nothing could be more erroneous than the notion that children *always* tell the truth. Although you won't hear many authorities on child training say it in so many words, most acknowledge in one way or another that children are sinners like the rest of us. Every parent knows that lying comes naturally to kids, so that up to age five or six, it is common for them to lie to make their lives easier, to escape blame, to avoid punishment, and, sometimes, just to make events more interesting.

In homes where high value is placed on morality, the first whopper told by four-year-old Sammy may cause great consternation. Not only because Sammy's early lies are apt to be easy to spot efforts to avoid responsibility ("I saw a monster come into the basement and pour your laundry soap all over the floor!"), but because real freedom in relationships comes when people speak the truth in love toward one another. Sammy's parents fear that Sammy might turn out to be a pathological liar for life.

You Must Not Underestimate Lying

While there is no need for parents to become alarmed over the early efforts of a child to evade responsibility by telling lies, it *is* hard to exaggerate the importance of truth in relationships with children. Nothing undermines trust like the discovery that your child has been fabricating in important matters: telling you he bought something when he stole it; assuring you that he's been attending classes when he was actually on the street with unsavory friends; insisting he's up-to-date with homework when he knows he's going to get an *F* in the course for his failure to complete any of the assignments. How can you maintain a close, loving relationship with someone you can't trust—ever? Yes, training your child to tell the truth is basic.

Nonetheless, there is no need to get upset and assume the worst at the child's early efforts at lying to escape trouble. Most children usually stop lying to escape blame by the time they start school. By age six or seven, Sammy finally discovers he hasn't succeeded in persuading anybody with his "whoppers."

Your part in this, however, is to punish lying when it occurs. Let us repeat, there is no need to push panic buttons when your preschooler lies. But it's equally critical for you to let the child know you're not buying his story, and to punish him for telling it.

Distinguishing Lying From Playful Creative Imagination

Before we tell you in detail how to stop lying behavior, we want to pay attention to one type of fabrication we don't consider lying. It occurs in young children and differs from lying in that the child doesn't do it to vindicate himself or to escape punishment for anything. Here, the child is using his imagination creatively for the fun of it. *He saw a big scaly dinosaur in the backyard. His playmate this morning was a turtle. He heard a monster in the basement* (but shows no real fear). Here you can play along with him, even chiming in with your own inventions. Don't squelch this stuff: It's vital for the development of imagination and creativity, and the child knows you know it's all in fun.

How to React When Your Child Lies

Three-year-old Ethan came to the kitchen where his father, Eric, was drying dishes. "Daddy, I just saw a big man with a black beard go to the bathroom on the floor in our basement!" he said with wide-eyed solemnity. Ethan's pants were wet.

"It bothers me a lot when you tell me things that aren't true," Eric replied. "You'll have to go to time out and stay there for two time-outs—one for wetting your pants, and the second for lying. First, I want you to change your pants, then take a rag and clean up the basement. After that, go to double time out."

You might want to learn from Eric's reaction to Ethan's lie.

First, Eric proceeded on the evidence in front of him. He knew the story was completely implausible, as toddlers' first efforts at exculpating themselves are likely to be. Ethan's pants were wet and Ethan's explanation for the puddle on the floor was "far out." So Eric made no further bones about whether or not his son was lying. Where you have factual evidence, proceed on the basis of it. Your child will quickly discover that you know when he's lying.

Second, Eric did not try to get Ethan to "confess." Some parents attempt to get their children to back off a lie by asking questions: "Did you make the puddle yourself, Ethan?" or "Come on, tell me the truth. Who *really* made the puddle?" or "There's no way a stranger could have gotten into our basement, now, is there Ethan?" Or "How did your pants get wet if you didn't do it?" Such attempts to extort confessions usually backfire and may lead to more lying: "But I saw the man. He sneaked in the window!" Or "No, Daddy, I didn't make the puddle. The man did." Or "One time a man came into Jimmy's basement and made a puddle on the floor!" Or "My pants got wet when I washed my hands and the water spilled on me."

It hurts when a child lies to you. And it's also frightening. You may see visions of yourself trying to cope with a habitually dishonest teenager in the future. Or you may feel pain from the violation of your close relationship with him. If you have the evidence, proceed right into expressing your feelings about the fact that the child has lied to you: "I really feel bad when you tell lies." Or "I don't like it at all when you make up things that aren't so."

Punish the misdeed *and* the lie. You can use double time out, as Eric did. Or you can remove privileges like this: "You will have to pass up watching TV tonight for wetting your pants, and you won't be able to have Jimmy over after dinner for telling me a lie about it." Or if you are using tokens or points, "You will lose four points right now, two for wetting and two for telling me a lie."

When You Can't Be Certain

The vase was broken. Connie knew that while she was downstairs loading the washer, little Valerie had been in the room by herself. She also knew Buttons, the Siamese house cat, had been restless lately and had been caught walking on the sideboard just a day or two earlier. She asked Valerie if she had broken the vase. Valerie denied having anything to do with it. "It just fell down," she told her mother.

What should Connie do? Should she try to worm a confession out of her daughter? Was it possible that the cat had knocked the vase onto the floor? Yes, it was. Maybe she could catch Valerie by getting her to admit to playing with things on the sideboard. But maybe she couldn't. What would you do?

Our recommendation is that you do *nothing*. When you don't *know* from the evidence that your child is lying, it's best not to try to trick her or force her into confessing because if she's lying you may and very likely will only get more lies. Children rarely confess.

If your uncertainty occurs about older children and habitual behavior, institute procedures for finding out the facts. For instance, if an older child has been caught lying again and again about class attendance or homework or progress in school, work out a program with the teacher by which you get factual feedback every day if necessary. Will the teacher sign a slip to be brought home daily certifying that Jerry really attended? Or that his homework was completed and handed in? Do whatever is necessary to get the facts.

And don't trust a habitual liar as a source for the facts. You must have a reliable basis for rewarding or punishing. If you don't, let it go. We don't like letting lying go, but there is no way to deal with it unless you know the truth! So make every effort to arrange things so you can know the truth and react appropriately. Habitual lying is too serious and has too many negative consequences for you to take it lightly.

When You Know the Truth About the Lie

When you do know the truth, confront the child with your strong negative feelings about his lying to you and its bad effect on your relationship. "It hurts me that I can't trust you because you have repeatedly told me what isn't so." "I feel really bad when you do that because I can't have the trust I want to have in you." Then punish the child appropriately.

By the same token, reward truth-telling in situations where you can see clearly that the child could lie to save himself from punishment but elects to tell the truth instead. By all means, give the punishment, but also reward the truth-telling. "I'm going to take away your TV privileges for this evening [or fine you so-and-so many tokens or points] for doing it. But I am really proud of you for telling me you did what I'd told you not to do. It must have been hard for you to tell me. I want to do something nice for you for telling me the truth even when it hurt. So I'm going to let you have an extra treat after dessert tonight." Or if you are using tokens or points: "I'm going to give you five extra points for telling me the truth."

Whatever You Do, Deal With Lying

You may want to pretend your child hasn't lied to you when you know for certain that he has. You may feel so bad you just want to forget it and hope it won't happen again. Don't give in to these very understandable feelings. Get the facts and then punish lying. In the case of an older child who lies about something concerning which you have no evidence, find out how to verify his story if you suspect lying. If you can't, you probably can't do anything about it. But wherever possible, set up an arrangement by which you can know the truth so you can act to remove any brief advantage gained from lying.

A Habit of Truth

When your child lies, calm down, think carefully, and get the facts. Once you are clear on the facts, don't panic. Punish the child. If the lie involves a transgression, punish for both the transgression *and for the lie*. If your four-year-old makes up creative stories playfully, don't react as if it's lying. Play along, do it yourself, and enjoy! But if the tale has obviously been created to get the child off the hook for some wrongdoing or to evade responsibility, punish the child for it. Nip lying in the bud. It's much easier than waiting until it's become an ingrained habit.

Mostly, focus on the positive goal—that is, developing in your child the "habit of truth." Since we serve a God who is the Father of truth, you can be sure you have an all-powerful parent on your side, empowering you, and full of compassion for your child.

17

Stealing

One of the less enjoyable moments in the work of a psychologist is the first meeting with a child who has been sent in to be "straightened out." Across the room sits a sullen, scowling preteen or adolescent. You don't have to be an extra talented clinician to read the scene before you even hear his answer to your first question: "What brings you in to see me today?"

Sometimes he just shrugs his shoulders: "I dunno. Ask my mom."

When the story unfolds, it might turn out that the youngster has taken something belonging to someone else—or, more likely, he has a habit of stealing. It is believed by many of the uninitiated that the psychologist or the pastor or the counselor can cure stealing (or lying or other misbehavior) by "using psychology on him" or by "finding out why he did it." We hope this book gains a wide circulation if for no other reason than to propagate the truth: Nobody can eliminate your child's behavior problems by cleverly talking with him. We may be able to help *you* do it, but the buck stops with you, not with a pastor, or a psychologist, or a youth worker!

How to Handle a Child's Stealing

Most kids steal, once or twice. Is there any parent who hasn't discovered filched bubblegum, stolen cookies, or a shoplifted toy in a child's grasp? Didn't you yourself once try to get away with taking something from a store or your parents' dresser drawer when you were four or five? Did your parents catch you? What did they do?

Candy made a venture into thievery at age four, and her mother made her march right back to the store, hand the stolen treasure to the grocer, and say, "I'm sorry I took this chewing gum without paying for it." Wisely, the grocer took the matter seriously, accepted the contraband, returned it solemnly to the display box, and told Candy he would not call the police unless she repeated the offense. Not likely— but the very mention of police terrified Candy. Ever after, she has paid in full for all her purchases.

If your child takes something that doesn't belong to him—don't pass it over as a cute little prank, don't smile indulgently. Take the matter seriously, and at the same time don't go off the deep end!

When a younger child takes an article that doesn't belong to him:

- Ask yourself whether you're certain he knows the difference between things belonging to him and the property of someone else. Children don't come by this distinction automatically, and until some point in the fourth or fifth year they may not understand it. They regard everything as their own property as a matter of course.
- Try not to leave money or other tempting property lying around. Tell the child specifically that he is not to take things others have put down without permission. It's possible he has never been explicitly informed about the importance of the distinction between what is his and what belongs to someone else.
- Don't avoid correct terminology in favor of euphemisms. Not: "You helped yourself to it." But: "You stole it," or "That's shoplifting." Call the act what it is.
- When you are faced with the fact that your child has

stolen something, take action. It isn't productive or wise to give the child a kind of "third degree" to obtain his admission that he did, indeed, steal. He may and probably will add lying to his stealing. Instead, tell him the facts as you see them, label the child's behavior as *wrong*, and insist that he return the stolen article, and that he work off debts incurred from the theft. Remember to punish him appropriately.

- Make him take responsibility for his action by returning or paying for what he took. If necessary, work with him on a plan whereby he can *earn* the money to repay his obligation. Accompany him when he goes to return the stolen article or arrange to make amends.

Although it's important to deal with stealing seriously, to make the child face his action as wrong and rectify what he has done, don't harp on it. After it's been resolved, drop it and leave it there. The likelihood is that he won't try it again. Take appropriate measures and the matter will usually come to an end.

When an Older Child Steals

With older children, stealing is less common and more serious. It's very important for you to act effectively if you discover it. If she suddenly turns up with a new possession or has money to spend you didn't supply and she didn't earn, get suspicious, look into the matter, but *don't cross-examine her*. If she claims someone gave her the thing or money as a gift, ask that person if it's true. If the other person denies your child's claim, confront her and go into action. If you discover money missing from your purse and she's suddenly wealthy, if nobody else could possibly have raided your cache, don't try to trip her up into confessing; confront her with the facts and act.

Label the behavior stealing, make her return the stolen object or money or work to repay it, and punish her. Do *not* send her to the pastor or a psychologist or another person to "have a talk with her" and do *not* simply talk with her yourself. The longer the lecture the more chance there is of reinforcing her with attention rather than effectively weakening the stealing behavior.

Although you shouldn't give her a lecture or settle for "having a talk with her," it's obvious that you will have some talking to do. What should you say? Tell her how you feel. "I feel very sad and angry when you do things that are wrong. This is wrong."

If you have discovered evidence of several similar episodes, it's important that you act effectively *each time*. It's especially important that you get information from other sources than the child. Look at facts, inquire, and when you see the evidence, act. Do not try to get the truth out of the child. Admittedly, you may not be aware of every transgression. There's nothing you can do about that. The older the child, the more of his life remains concealed from you. That's part of growing up.

When an episode of theft does come to your attention, you're likely to look for all sorts of farfetched explanations to avoid facing the facts. Most kids who are habitual stealers will be glad to help you do this. So don't ask them. Form your own conclusions and don't abet the child's lying by insisting on getting his admission of guilt before doing anything about the transgression.

Most important: When an episode is over, *forgive*. And drop it.

18

How (and When) to Talk

Do you talk with your children? Genuinely *talk* with them? We don't mean to ask whether you occasionally address some words in their direction. Do you *converse* with them? Do you *tell* them what the score is? Do you *explain* to them what you want? Do you *communicate* some of your inner self to them? Some parents don't realize relationships with children must involve *talking* with children. They may yell. They may speak words *at* their children. This is not the same thing as *talking with* them. Whether or not you talk with your children and the way you express yourself when you do can make a huge difference in your relationships. Furthermore, a lot can be deduced about your parenting effectiveness by observing the way you communicate with your offspring.

The Marks of Good "Parent Talk"

What makes children grow up feeling worthless? What generates low self-esteem? Of course, these phenomena may have any of a number of causes, but parents may make

162

an important contribution to the developing person's self-estimate.

How precisely can parents affect the child's self-view?

Well, most parents don't blatantly tell their children they are worthless, stupid, and utterly repulsive! Of course not! It's more subtle than that. And one of the subtleties is the *way* parents talk with their children.

Why not check yourself out on the following list of characteristics? We consider them descriptive of good parent-child communication. On how many of them does your conversation style meet the standards that get results? There is a space for you to check those qualities on which you think your talk with your children is exemplary. Those you don't check—well, you can begin today to discover the results you'll get if you begin them. They are all part of what we believe it means to *love* your children:

Marks of Good "Parent Talk"—A Checklist

☐ *Respect.* Effective, acceptable parental talk with children shows respect for children and conveys to them by its style and tone that they are valuable persons, created in God's image, and made a little lower than the angels. Contrary to the opinion of some parents, just because a human being is your child doesn't confer on you a license to talk abusively at him, to yell uncontrollably at him, or to put him down or insult him.

☐ *"I," not "You."* If your child hears nothing but accusing *"You"* sentences, she's likely to believe she's an awful person: "You complained all the way to school. You make me so mad!" *"You"* followed by a chewing out can easily be heard by a child as a parent's way of saying she's inferior. Instead, use *"I."* "I get angry when you complain so much." "I feel very uncomfortable when I see your room left so messy." "I feel bad when you talk to me like that and I want you to speak respectfully."

☐ *Avoid "Always" and "Never."* Adverbs like *always* and

never are over inclusive. "You *always* act like the rest of us have no rights." "You *never* think of anyone but yourself." Sentences like that may mean to the child, "You're a hopeless case. You can't act any other way." Much better to say, "Sometimes I feel as though you've forgotten that I have rights too."

☐ *The Action, not the Child.* Make clear that what you don't like is what the child has done or left undone, not the child himself. "I love you, but I don't like it when you . . ."

☐ *Truth.* Nor do you have any reason to mislead these individuals simply because they are innocent, naive, or young. You must learn to talk to them truthfully, taking time to explain things at their level rather than putting them off with clichés or deception.

What Shall We Tell Him?

Marvin and Tammy Secord enjoyed making plans with their five-year-old son Brent. They were delighted with the sparkle in his eye when they discussed going as a family to California to visit Grandpa and Grandma for their next vacation. They didn't make a promise, but they talked about the trip as if it was likely to take place. The child talked about the upcoming journey nearly every day.

But then the Secords were invited to join a group of young couples for a few days' camping. The group would pool their resources and their children and hire a sitter for all the kids together at one of the homes. The camping trip would be a blast! They wanted so much to go. But how could they tell Brent? They finally hit on a plan. They would tell him they couldn't afford the trip to California. They would impress on him the value of money and show him how very expensive airplane tickets would be. They would remind him that they hadn't made a firm promise. And they were sure he would accept the explanation. They couldn't tell him they simply chose to abandon their plans to travel to California with him in order to do something that would be much more fun for them.

What would *you* have advised this couple to do? We probably would have suggested they consider joining the crowd for their next camping trip and following through on the California trip that was so important to Brent. But given that they would not be willing to do that, we surely would have suggested to this couple that they tell Brent the truth, even though they weren't particularly proud of their own actions. Brent might have cause to be terribly disappointed, but he would have no cause to see his parents as liars, or to learn by their example that the best way to get out of a tight spot is to lie.

We don't maintain that there is *never* a time to protect your child from certain raw truths he isn't mature enough to digest. But we do suggest that you avoid lying to any child. You may choose to give him only limited information because he can't grasp the truth in its fullness. Or—and maybe this is even better—you can often make use of unpleasant facts to teach your child proper values.

Do not threaten. When you have made your request clear or explained a rule plainly to a child, never threaten! Not even once! You may dispassionately and clearly spell out what the child can expect as a consequence of doing what you want or of disobeying. But then be prepared to administer the promised consequences. Plan punishment you are going to be willing to employ, like time out or deprivation of privileges or, if the situation warrants it, a spanking. Although you will *never* threaten, you may make clear *once* what the consequences of violating a rule will be, but do not present it as a threat to prompt a misbehaving child.

We realize now that when we were raising our four children, our threatening was a mistake. We did it to protect ourselves from having to face the unpleasant task of carrying out consequences. Parents threaten because they hate to do anything for which the child will resent them. Or they hesitate to inject unpleasantness into a situation they did so want to be beautiful. So they hope that a threat will work and they won't have to do anything pleasant.

Some parents threaten twice—or three, four, five, six times. Usually their children know just how far they can stretch the "threats only" mode and they push it to the limit. They can do this because children become experts regarding parental threats. They develop the ability to read each parent's facial expressions and voice patterns with great accuracy. And they can calculate precisely how many threats will be issued before the situation becomes truly risky.

Act *immediately*. Teach your child that you mean what you say, and that you won't use threats or scoldings to intimidate. When you have made this all clear, be sure to follow through.

Parents who threaten and then fail to act according to their threats create a situation where the child learns not to take the parental message seriously. Such parents are actually training the child not to obey them.

Do not "have a talk with him" as a consequence. Frequently, parents complain to us about their children's misbehavior: "Tommy keeps hitting his sister. I just don't know what to do about it!" Regularly, we ask, "What did you do when he last hit her?" As often as not the parent answers, "Why, I had a talk with him and I got my spouse to have a talk with him! We both explained to him how important it is for him to treat his sister nicely." "Well," we respond, "you just showed us why Tommy keeps hitting his sister. You are rewarding him for it. A talk is not punishment, it's a reward." Many parents, if they kept close tabs on Tommy's behavior, would learn that, in fact, their talks only increased the frequency of Tommy's sister-slugging.

"Having a talk" is actually reinforcing. Parental attention is one of the most rewarding things you can give to a child. It's one of the things every child wants the most from parents. No way is it a punishment, and no way can you expect talking with your child to curb bad behavior.

Talk to children when they are good. Talk with your child, yes, but do it at the time many parents never choose to talk with their children—when they do something *right*! As someone put it, "Catch 'em being good," and then give them loving attention. Many parents think, "Janey's not bothering anyone right now. Let sleeping dogs lie. I'm not going to disturb her and stir up trouble." As a result, the only time they show Janey any attention is when she's teasing the dog, tormenting her little brother, or littering the house. When you notice that your child has been good, say you'd like to sit down with her and tell her what you've especially appreciated about her behavior. Ask her what you can do for her to show her how very much you do appreciate it. Then do it. Always follow through on promised benevolences as well as punishments.

Talk to children about God. Talk to your child about the most important things in life. It's so easy to think of your children in terms of what you ought to be getting them to do or not do (Has he done his chores? Is he spending enough time on his homework? Is she eating too much sugar for proper nutrition? Are her fingernails clean? How can I get him to rest? What about grooming?) But these matters, important as they are, cannot give any meaning to life or relationships. So discover the priceless results you will get from talking with your child about your faith and spiritual reality.

Ask your child to think about matters of eternal significance. Ask her questions to get her to think: "If Jesus were to visit us, what do you think He would talk about at the dinner table?" "If we could see God, what do you think He would look like?" "How do you think God can be here with us when He's also with Grandma and Grandpa in Australia?"

Don't use God as a threat! God isn't your whip. Do not use "God talk" for punishment. Don't "use" God to control your child's behavior:

"Don't you know the fourth commandment says you have to obey me?"

"God will punish you if you don't do as I say."

"Remember, God is watching you! He'll get you if you lie."

"Do you think Jesus would like you to watch that TV show?"

When Martin, our oldest, was three, we discovered we were making this very mistake. We regularly exhorted him to share his toys with his little sister, Annie, because he was a Christian "and Christians share their toys with others." One day he came in from playing with the boy next door, saying, "Dad, will you please go over and tell Mattie he has to let me use his wagon because he's a Christian like I'm not!" All we'd accomplished was to make our kid think nobody in his right mind would want to be a Christian if all it means is that you have to give up your things to others!

Tell your child what you want from him. Talk with the child about what you want him to do. Many parents *think* they have done this when they haven't. Or they have not done it well. There are some important points to follow:

Be specific. Don't say, "Take care of the dog," but "I want you to give Toby two cups of dry dog food and fill his water dish every morning before you come to the table."

Be courteous. Not "For cryin' out loud, can't you give me a little help around here?" But, "Will you please come here and help me by setting the table?"

Be straightforward, not indirect. Not: "Why doesn't anybody in this house ever close a door?" But: "Jerry, I would like you to close the door, please."

Make clear and simple rules, and tell your child exactly what they are. Formulate rules by agreement with other adults in home: two parents, or parent and grandparent, or parent and roommate must formulate the rules together if they are supposed to help train the child. As the child becomes capable of it, you can permit him to participate in rule formulation. But remain clear in the head: You are the boss, he isn't. Participation doesn't mean taking over. The rules, when finally formulated, may have involved negotiation, but they are still *your* rules. So when all is said and done, you must tell the child clearly what the rules are. Clearly and specifically.

Not: "From now on I want you to get to bed without so much delay." But: "I will tell you when it's bedtime. When I do, I want you to _____ then I'll come and pray with you and kiss you good-night and turn off the light. After the light is off, I don't want you to get out of bed or call me again."

Not nagging or yelling: "I've *told* you a million times to come to the table when you're called! What *am* I going to *do* with you?" Some parents almost never address a child as a person. Instead they holler, scream, shriek, bellow, roar, shout, nag, lecture.

These are hard habits to break, because children reinforce parents for doing them. Actually, nagging, yelling and lecturing "work" in that they eventually get the child's attention or make a kind of impression on him, and he will do what you want. That's the problem: The child reinforces these damaging behaviors.

But it won't last.

Talk with your child about things that interest him. Converse with him. Show interest. If you're not interested in what interests your child, try to find a way to get involved and get interested.

Share your thoughts, your interests, and your activities with your child. Few adults actually *tell* children about themselves, instead they confine themselves to asking the child questions about the child's affairs. It's an excellent thing to discuss the child's interests with her, but take time as well to share *your* world, *your* feelings, *your* interests too. Tell her about things that interest you. "I have always liked to take cars apart and see why they can run and fix them too if anything goes wrong. It's fun for me to work on engines. What's the most fun for you?

Get her and you *thinking* together about things. "I wonder what it would be like if everybody could fly. What would be good about it? What might be bad about it?" "What would it be like if all the toys in the stores were free for boys and girls? What would be good about that? Can you think of anything that might not be so good about it?" "What would it be like if all the trees were just as tall as you and no bigger?" "What if we had twenty boys and girls in our family? What would happen? What would be good about having so many brothers and sisters? What would be harder?" "What would it be like if we could see God the way we see each other? What would be good about that? What would be bad about it?" Talk with him about what he is doing. Get down on your knees on the floor with him and say, "Is this a castle you're building? Tell me about it. Does someone live there?" Get involved in the child's play and work.

When a child initiates a conversation, don't brush it off, saying something like, "Well, how about that?—Dinner will be ready soon. Wash your hands and face." *Converse. Ask. Tell. Listen.*

Talk positively as you give the child reinforcers. Please bear with this reminder: Talk as you administer rewards, so that your approval and smile become paired with whatever concrete reinforcer you're giving. That way, your approval and your smile will become the most rewarding things in the world to your child. "I am so pleased with the way you behaved at the table when we had company! I want to make some cookies just for you. What kind would you like the most?" "You've been so obedient lately, doing everything I have asked you to do without arguing or complaining or putting it off. I'm really excited about how you've done it. I'd like to let you choose the dessert for tonight's dinner. What's your favorite?"

Are you already using some of the characteristics of positive parent talk? We expect it's very unlikely you've checked them all unless you are either perfect or capable of kidding yourself. More commonly, parents will find they need to improve the way they talk with their children. The bonus they'll discover is that talking with these wonderful little creatures (or, later, fascinating big creatures) is easy, powerful—and rewarding!

One final thought: Don't just talk—*do*! Make sure your own behavior is above reproach. Resist the temptation to say "finders keepers" and pocket the excessive change the cashier accidentally gave you. Don't lie, twist the truth, or take advantage of others. *Do the behaviors you're trying to train your child to perform!*

Let your own sterling behavior interpret the meaning of what you are trying to tell your child to be and do.

In closing, we'd like to encourage you to make the important commitment today. Determine in your heart that you can train your children to honor, respect, and obey. Determine that you will begin the work of training for *their* sake, as well as your own.

Very soon, the work of parenting will become the joy you've hoped it would be. How about it?—Start your own program today, and join the ranks of *empowered* parents!

The Center for Christian Psychological Services receives numerous requests for referrals to licensed Christian professional counselors who use Christian cognitive therapy as set forth in Dr. Backus' books. The Center would be happy to receive from you a brief summary of your counseling experience with misbelief therapy and your qualifications, license status, and commitment to Christian truth in your practice. On the basis of such information, the Center will refer callers from your area to you. Please include a telephone number with area code, address, and the name of the facility with which you are affiliated.

The Center for Christian Psychological Services
Roseville Professional Center #435
2233 N. Hamline
St. Paul, Minnesota 55113
(612) 633–5290

WEEK OF _____   BEHAVIOR CHART FOR _____

New Behavior Description	Point Value	ONE HASH MARK FOR EACH EPISODE							Point Total
		SUN	MON	TUE	WED	THU	FRI	SAT	
POINTS EARNED THIS WEEK									
POINT BALANCE CARRIED FORWARD FROM LAST WEEK									
TOTAL POINTS EARNED									

Undesirable Behavior Description	Point Value	ONE HASH MARK FOR EACH EPISODE							Point Total
		SUN	MON	TUE	WED	THU	FRI	SAT	
TOTAL POINTS LOST THIS WEEK									

TOTAL POINTS AVAILABLE (points earned minus points lost)	

Privileges For Points	Point Value	ONE HASH MARK FOR EACH EPISODE							Point Total
		SUN	MON	TUE	WED	THU	FRI	SAT	
TOTAL POINTS USED FOR PRIVILEGES THIS WEEK									
POINT BALANCE (points available minus points used)									